The Loves of My Life

BY THE SAME AUTHOR

Forgetting Elena: A Novel
The Joy of Gay Sex (co-authored)
Nocturnes for the King of Naples: A Novel
States of Desire: Travels in Gay America
A Boy's Own Story: A Novel
Caracole: A Novel
The Darker Proof: Stories from a Crisis (co-authored)
The Beautiful Room Is Empty
Genet: A Biography
The Burning Library: Essays
Our Paris: Sketches from Memory
Skinned Alive: Stories
The Farewell Symphony: A Novel
Marcel Proust: A Life
The Married Man: A Novel
The Flâneur: A Stroll Through the Paradoxes of Paris
Fanny: A Fiction
Arts and Letters: Essays
My Lives: A Memoir
Chaos: A Novella and Stories
Hotel de Dream: A New York Novel
Rimbaud: The Double Life of a Rebel
City Boy: My Life in New York During the 1960s and '70s
Sacred Monsters: New Essays on Literature and Art
Jack Holmes and His Friend: A Novel
Inside a Pearl: My Years in Paris
Our Young Man: A Novel
The Unpunished Vice: A Life of Reading
A Saint from Texas: A Novel
A Previous Life: A Novel
The Humble Lover: A Novel
The Spirit Lamp: a Forthcoming Novel

The Loves of My Life

A Sex Memoir

Edmund White

BLOOMSBURY PUBLISHING
LONDON • OXFORD • NEW YORK • NEW DELHI • SYDNEY

BLOOMSBURY PUBLISHING
Bloomsbury Publishing Plc
50 Bedford Square, London, WC1B 3DP, UK
29 Earlsfort Terrace, Dublin 2, Ireland

BLOOMSBURY, BLOOMSBURY PUBLISHING and the Diana logo
are trademarks of Bloomsbury Publishing Plc

First published in 2025 in the United States by Bloomsbury USA
First published in Great Britain 2025

Some names and details of individuals have been changed to preserve their anonymity

A catalogue record for this book is available from the British Library

ISBN: HB: 978-1-5266-8670-1; EBOOK: 978-1-6397-3373-6; EPDF: 978-1-5266-9127-9

2 4 6 8 10 9 7 5 3 1

Typeset by Westchester Publishing Services
Printed and bound in Great Britain by CPI Group (UK) Ltd, Croydon CR0 4YY

FSC
www.fsc.org
MIX
Paper | Supporting responsible forestry
FSC® C171272

To find out more about our authors and books visit www.bloomsbury.com and sign up for our newsletters

To Rick Whitaker

Mae West hearing a bad actress auditioning for West's hit comedy Sex: *"She's flushin' my play down the terlet!"*

AUTHOR'S NOTE

The names of individuals who are identified in this book by first name only have been anonymized and certain key details have been fictionalized. Any resemblance between a fictionalized individual and a real person with the same name is strictly coincidental.

PREFACE

In my novels and memoirs I have written quite a bit about sex, even very outré sex. I've always insisted I've approached sex as a realist, not as a pornographer. That is, I like to represent what goes on through someone's mind while having sex—the idle thoughts, the resentful thoughts, the comic aspects of the body failing to meet the acrobatic ambitions of the imagination—and the sometimes enriching, sometimes embarrassing or dull, often distracting or irrelevant or wonderfully intimate and tender moments of lovemaking.

I'm at an age when writers are supposed to say finally what mattered most to them—for me it would be thousands of sex partners.

There is still a prudishness about sex, not only in America but everywhere. Sex and comedy are the two subjects that are never taken seriously, though we think about sex constantly—and about comedy periodically, if we're lucky, if only in the form of self-satire. I suppose prudishness guarantees paternity, so crucial in keeping bloodlines pure.

Gay men have seldom been candid about their sex lives and are even less so now that they are getting married and fathering offspring. Paternity is not the problem for them, so much as respectability. Internet anonymity has facilitated new possibilities of "cheating" and hypocrisy.

* * *

IT MAY SEEM ABSURD FOR an octogenarian to be writing a sex memoir, but it could be argued that he has decades of experience to draw on and an unimpeachable point of view even if the horse he has in the race may have become feeble and cobbled. Because I am in my eighties, have *most* of my marbles, been a practicing gay since age thirteen, lived through the oppression of the 1950s, the post-Stonewall exaltation of the 1970s and the wipeout after the advent of AIDS in the 1980s, the discovery of the lifesaving therapies of the 1990s, the granting of gay marriage equal rights in the States in 2015, the parallel right to adopt children, the brewing storm in the 2020s against everything labeled "woke" (trans people, drag, books, puberty-delaying drugs)—because I've witnessed all this drama and melodrama, I'm perfectly situated to view how we got here.

I've seen gays go from thinking they're neurotic to what we call Pride. In the 1950s, no matter how much fun we were having there was always a moment in a gay soirée when one of us would look around balefully but with a giggle and say, "Gosh, we're sick. Just a bunch of sick queens." Now we're star athletes, bullying businessmen, Latin crooners. Whereas half a century ago gays preferred individual sports (tennis, swimming) to team sports (football, rugby), were afraid of corporations, and chose even humble trades (leather tooling) to anything in groups. Recently I was privileged to be invited to an elite dinner of gay men, four of whom said they loved corporate life in New York and felt very fulfilled. I worked in public relations for a ghastly corporation in the seventies at which I was told a famous photographer I'd proposed to do the portraits of the countless vice presidents was too effeminate to go onto the fifty-sixth floor, where the all-male white executives had their offices, each guarded by a female secretary.

In the 1940s gay men wanted sex with straights (including drunk sailors who beat them up afterward), and just a hint of shared homosexual desire detected in the other person could spoil a trick—as *Giovanni's Room* demonstrates. Now we have a friendlier version of that—we fall for opposites if gay and strive to turn them into twins. If we succeed, we stop having sex with them (it's called lesbian crib death). I don't know why I made "Latin crooners" an example, but aren't they supposed to be lady-killers? With patent leather hair smelling of violets? Anyway, they're gay now, too.

If gays have gone from invisibility to ubiquity and from self-hatred to self-acceptance, we should also recognize we're still being pushed off cliffs in Yemen—and from the top fronds of Florida palms, for all I know. One in five Generation Zers identify as LGBTQ+, which might seem like progress, but nearly half are contemplating suicide and 70 percent are reporting they're severely anxious. Presumably young straights are less at risk, but those are figures we, as good scientists, should verify.

When I was young, gays were given funerals when they turned thirty. Your life was finished. You had to be thin, wearing Top-Siders and blue cashmere sweaters, you had to make broad gestures and be a big Cam, you had to have your hair bleached and straightened in the surfer look. Now we have daddies, chubbies, chasers, twinks, twink tops, feeders, gainers, spankers, voyeurs, and exhibitionists, not to mention asexuals and males whose genitals are kept in chastity cages or who themselves are kept naked in real cages and fed from a dog bowl. Some gay men have hair on their backs and even their chests. Then there are the adult babies with their Pride mega-diapers and adult swim diapers, extra-large training pants and giant pacifiers. And the furries . . .

All this is what is meant by "diversity."

In my own case, Eros at least crashed through class barriers. I seduced or hired men of all creeds, races, and ages, though irrationally I favored the young. Had I run after older men with some power and wealth, I might now be in a less precarious position financially, or at least I might better understand the world, as Gore Vidal suggested when he argued we should all read Louis Auchincloss because he wrote about Wall Street winners and their ways. Not that I haven't had sex with many old, obese men. I used to think I could have been in a harem since I could find any roly-poly pasha sexy. I could find at least one square inch somewhere that was desirable, or more likely a dramatic role that would excite me, so I could be like Kit in *The Sheltering Sky*, who escapes her rescuers and gratefully returns to captivity in a harem to be kept on drugged sherbets, her veiled beauty endlessly available and demeaned.

* * *

WHY DO PEOPLE HAVE SEX? Is sex the desperate, passionate thing it was in the past? Do young people fast, weep, threaten suicide, as they once did until they knew if their love was returned or if they would get dumped? Do poets have their hearts broken as of yore? Is "crystallization" (Stendhal's idea that if a horny teen just hears the word *love* spoken in the presence of his ravishing, wonderfully companionable aunt, he'll instantly be smitten) still in force? Was Rochefoucauld right that no one ever fell in love without first reading about it?

What goes on in people's heads when they have sex? Fear of a fiasco, delight in merging, yearning to dominate or succumb, hope for eternal love, cynical pleasure in duping a virgin, thereby adding a notch to their belt? Or just animal pleasure?

Is it a rite of passage ("You don't mean you're still a virgin!?")? Is it competitive ("Everyone says he's a hung top who can cum three times a night. Average body, but who cares? I like big meat not muscle Marys")?

I never experienced desire in its "pure" form; for me sex was always full of drama or affection. For instance, during the hormonal rush of adolescence, I was masturbating five times a day, even after constant "spanking the monkey" (as we used to say) had become painful and reduced the flow of semen to a mere drip. But every time I was running a movie in my head of someone, nine times out of ten a male, who cherished me, who sunk with ecstasy, who pledged eternal love, who joined me mentally and spiritually in a pinpoint of light. As a teen I wept over romantic movies, especially sad ones such as *Camille*, and well into my twenties I'd stare intensely at a man on the subway and wonder whether I could spend the rest of my life with him, despite the wen on his left cheek or his dubious taste in ties. I still go misty-eyed listening to 1940s ballads. Now when I look at a forty-year-old lawyer on television, I immediately wonder if he has a thick one, but as a youngster I never thought below the belt but just wondered if this man across from me on the A train might decide I was the perfect lifelong mate.

True to the values of the 1950s, I worried at seventeen that my youth and desirability were running out. At boarding school, I kept visiting the decade-older art academy students across the street and falling in love with three or four of them—one an emaciated abstract expressionist named Paul who seldom spoke but sweetly encouraged me to read him my translations from the *Aeneid* or Catullus and then discussed them. He committed suicide ten years later. Then there was a guy, a tall redhead, who made stained-glass panes, little abstract ones in wood frames suspended on wires before the window (he would be ninety now if still alive). He gave me one, which in my generalized despair I broke deliberately then crawled, sobbing, through the shards. I got straight A's and never made a scene and seemed almost normal, but in my single room I was fairly hysterical (in my Buddhist phase of intense meditation I even levitated an inch off my bed). I liked Buddhism because it led to the extinction of all desire, which in my case was noxious because it was beamed at members of my own sex, a longing I knew was bad if seemingly ineradicable.

My point is that for me sex was always linked to love, even during so-called anonymous sex. I fell in love ten times a day and still take the sappy lyrics of those old love ballads as wisdom. With complete earnestness I would read magazine articles on how to improve your marriage. Every time I went to a party when I was young, I thought I might meet the love of my life. Now parties are drudgery, or at least the prospect is grim. New people, banal conversation, someone trying to suss out how you might be of use . . .

Maybe when you're young, new in town, unfettered with previous entanglements, ready to blossom in the right soil, lonely, not on guard, when your opinions about politics and art and child-rearing and ecology and Republicans have not yet hardened into cement, when you're one unformed individual in search of another who smiles and touches you, when your heart is perhaps unprotected, then laughter and gentle questioning and cocktail refills and immediate conversational concessions and reciprocal erections in matching khakis can lead to stolen kisses and eventual merging and flaming hopes that this time it's for keeps, until you look around his apartment the next morning with a headache in need of surgery and find a few too many Hello Kitty plush dolls on their own shelf and the complete works of Ayn Rand.

But things have also changed for the better. Gays who are nest builders can now marry and have children, either adopted or born from surrogates. I know five such households and they all seem happy and flourishing. In progressive cities such as New York, Boston, San Francisco, and Los Angeles—and dozens of other college towns scattered across the country—these families are accepted without comment. These same-sex parents go to PTA meetings, host birthday parties, join car pools, share babysitters, help with homework. Sometimes they even go to church. One of my friends successfully adopted a gay fourteen-year-old whom no one wanted. (Most would-be parents are looking for babies, and as orphans get older they "age out.") The life-giving bother of children—their growing pains, their academic careers, their orthodontists, wardrobes, peer groups, athletic prowess, romantic fears and triumphs, their hobbies, sleepovers, their conformism, their rebellions, their addictions, their tuitions—every parent has signed a contract for years and years of this. And that contract binds them to their community, to the politics of the moment, to fads and slang and rap music, to censorship, to "wokeness," to visits to the zoo, concerts, France. As little children they can say "cute" things and display unexpected humor, tolerance, affection, irritability; sometimes they're rowdy or philosophical.

A ten-year old is curiously wise. At that age I wrote a manifesto saying that subteens should be given the vote, since only they were unswayed by candidates' looks, family name, marital status. Only a ten-year-old can judge the issues limpidly, I argued. At ten, I was eerily empathetic with older women, indifferent to most children, good at surviving, and in fact stealthily power mad (a school play held no interest for me unless I could be the king). Paradoxically, I've never thought I was good enough, unselfish enough, rich enough, or stable enough to raise children. But I look around at the happy families being raised by two women or two men (most of them, not incidentally, prosperous) and I envy them.

People keep asking me if I resent being labeled a gay writer. Admittedly the label puts off many straight readers, just as I suppose *Black fiction* used to put off many whites.

Of course we came to see Black fiction as quite simply some of our best. Imagine a world in which there were no Zora Neale Hurston or James Baldwin or Toni Morrison. In the same way imagine a world in which there were no Walt Whitman or Alan Hollinghurst or Proust or Henry James (whose "The Pupil" is one of the best gay short stories ever written, unless it's Conrad's "The Secret Sharer"—and he wasn't even gay!). True, heterosexual readers don't like encountering cocks and balls, but they are mercifully absent in James and Conrad.

Sex writing can seem foolish, especially to the English. They even give out an award for the most embarrassing sex writing of the year. Everyone from Walt Whitman to D. H. Lawrence has "shocked" them, though they usually say sex "bores them" (Freud tells us that boredom is a mild form of anxiety). I always feel as if I don't really know people unless I've gone to bed with them; in the same way I'm disappointed by novelists who leave out the sex scenes because they're embarrassing or "irrelevant" or technically too hard to write convincingly. It seems a pity that most feature films won't go beyond being "suggestive." Not only are we cheated from seeing our most beautiful contemporaries making love, we also don't witness a fundamental truth about the character—rough or tender, selfish or attentive, efficient or languorous, perfunctory or sweet.

I'm grateful to all the men who shared a pillow with me. Maybe it sounds pathetic, but gratitude has always been my primary response to sex. I wish I had been more bisexual and more open to other races and ages, though my record there is better than that of most white gay men of my generation. Grateful, yes, that these other people have given me if only for an hour their warm, sleek bodies, their lingering kisses and aggressive genital invasions. When I've felt, even when I was much, much younger, that I was no longer attractive and had crossed the line into invisibility, the sudden redemption of a *bon coup* (a "fine fuck" as the French say), the largesse of a Welsh waiter I met in Los Angeles or the generosity of a professional baseball player in Florida—the unexpected kindness of these guys restored me to another decade or two of self-respect in this endless life of mine.

First Lust

Although I have a small penis and entered puberty at the ordinary time, nevertheless I was stung from ten or eleven by sexual desire. It was a constant, nagging lust—or "hankering" as nineteenth-century translations of Buddhist texts call the general source of our attachment to the world, the longing that ties us to the wheel of endless rebirth, which Buddhists fear and the rest of us want.

I must have been in fifth grade and hence ten or eleven when I developed my maniacal attachment to Nick. He lived with his mother in a big wooden house in Evanston, Illinois. When you look at movies of the late 1940s and early 1950s, the houses were dowdy—warrens of many underfurnished rooms, their rugs dusty, pale blue wool, not fitting wall-to-wall (that error of taste came later) but stranded with a wide border of parquet on all four sides. Easy chairs with tilted lamps beside them. Everything in witless shades of brown. A huge and inefficient kitchen with shiny counters under narrow windows. Nothing remarkable, nothing stylish, a free-standing radio like an upended child's coffin.

Nick's mother was never around in the afternoons and mine didn't get home from work until six thirty. From three thirty to six we were alone in that big, boxy house, always overheated. Nick would go to the icebox and pour himself a glass of orange juice made from frozen concentrate, just as we made it in my house. I was intensely aware of him as he moved about and peeled off his sweater and threw it on the couch covered with scratchy wool faded in patches by the sunlight from a bright turquoise to a ghostly teal. He was small and very pale, his face as pretty as a girl's but too big for his body and made bigger by his carefully oiled and combed hair, a gleaming, immobile structure weighing him down like Hungary's hereditary crown. He had a small black mole on his neck and another on his right cheek, which gave him the look of an eighteenth-century woman with her beauty patches. His eyes were small and black. His lips should've been rosy but they were bloodless, almost blue, wet.

We would wrestle for hours, not out of hostility or competitiveness but because it felt good—to rub our crotches against each other, to have my biceps pinned down by his knees and inhale the odor of his piss-stained denim jeans. I didn't think Nick's mother washed his jeans more than once a month, and after weeks of wear they had a lovely history, a funk that you would have noticed only if you had your nose buried in his crotch, as I did. We were clueless young boys; we didn't wear deodorant or shower often and we wiped only in the morning in the most cursory way. Sometimes our breath smelled of tuna or peanut butter or Tootsie Rolls.

But Nick's glands were pine knots waiting to be lit and even now quietly dripping oil; his arms and legs were small and round and compact; if you cut them in half, they would be round at every point. His cheeks were as charged with color as the heart of the peony, as florid as his lips were pale. Even in the strongest sunlight his face betrayed no fuzz no matter how soft or pale. It was as smooth and matte as talc. His voice hadn't changed from its high, silver, Magnificat clarity. He was strong and fearless and though much smaller than I, he usually won in wrestling. I should say "wrestling" since I was obviously playing another sort of sport, a zero-sum game that meant we were always in each other's arms, breathing hard, turning and twisting. It was a game I aimed to lose and that I contested only enough to keep it going, pinned down, denim in my face. When we long for something, say a cock, we fetishize what guards and disguises that thing, blue jeans and their metal grommets. I was a jeans fanatic.

Maybe a year later—or could it have been six months? Youth has only two dates, the beginning of school and the end—I invited Nick to spend the night. I suspect such an invitation seemed pretty weird. As casual sounding as I could, I said, "Come over for a pajama party. My mom will make us dinner, we'll watch some TV [still a novelty then], and you can stay over and we'll drive you back in the morning."

I wonder now how it was all arranged. My mother was always filled with such inchoate desires—for my father to remarry her; for the bruiser on the next barstool to buy her another highball; for Mr. Preston, the rich guy she'd met on the plane and who'd invited her to his mansion in Santa Barbara, to ask her back for another "romantic" (i.e. sexual) weekend—that maybe she recognized in me my equally insistent and incoherent desires. She didn't approve of homosexuality—who could have in 1951?—but desire, if it remained undiagnosed, unnamed, pure and all-consuming, spoke to her, to her innermost heart. She went along with my request, especially since I'd known Nick since second grade, four whole years ago. Our friendship was consecrated by time. Besides, I didn't have many other friends, or arguably any! My mother didn't want to discourage my burgeoning amicability. Even at that age I agreed with William Blake that it was better to strangle an infant in its crib than nurse an unacted desire.

Once Nick and I had eaten the bland pork cutlets and brussels sprouts my mother prepared, along with tall glasses of milk and Oreos for dessert, after we'd watched *Your Hit Parade* on TV, in which nearly the same hit songs recycled week after week, each time produced with a new theme, new sets, and new dances, so that one week Rosemary Clooney's "If I Knew You Were Comin', I'd've Baked a Cake" featured a solo dancer in a housedress and an apron bending before an oven and the next week a mustache-twirling French chef in a white toque unboxing a tiered wedding cake to the surprise of a cavorting couple. Nick and I watched that with dulled fascination as my fish eyes kept stealing sidelong glances at his child-like body. Soon I hoped it would be unwrapped like a mysterious Christmas present.

In my room I had twin beds that formed an L in one corner and wooden chairs and a knotty-pine desk and burlap curtains and brown corduroy bedspreads, the oblong of each upper mattress outlined in brown piping.

We stripped down to our underpants (I studied his crotch—no tenting) and climbed in bed. I said, "Good night," and he mumbled something and I turned off the bedside lamp. The room was electric with the sort of suspense the victim's family feels before the verdict.

I couldn't sleep. As my eyes adjusted to the dark, I could make out the outlines of Nick's face, usually crowned by black unguent-heavy hair. Was he awake?

Was that the sound of his eyelids batting against the pillow?

Finally I couldn't stand it any longer. I leapt out of bed without a plan, approached his bed, retreated, said hoarsely, "You awake?"

And he peeped, "Yes."

"Can I sit on your bed and talk a minute?"

"Sure." He sounded dubious and drew the word out experimentally.

I sat down and could feel the presence of his leg through the covers but he wasn't moving it; it was a stone. I was at the age (and would be for many years) when all my desires felt, necessarily, reciprocated, as though the high wattage of my longing sparked an equal interest in the object of that desire, though in reality there was often nothing in the other person but indignation or indifference.

Was he lying there with a hard-on as rigid as mine? Was he frustrated by his own shyness and wondering why it was taking me so long to make the first move? Was he aching to be jacked off?

Propelled by my fantasy of reciprocal desire, I reached under the covers and felt his penis. He turned on the light, threw off the covers, wriggled out of his underwear. He hadn't gone through puberty yet! I felt as if I'd dipped into the holy chalice and there was no blood turning into wine.

We never mentioned my midnight attack and soon we'd gone back to our companionable wrestling, though every afternoon I quickly wearied of our exercises now that I knew there was no drowned treasure at the bottom of the well.

I just wrote a poem in memory of those days:

When we're twelve, the faces of friends are strong
as
Symbols—but of what? We scarcely look at adults,
who are all
Elbows and irritation, but our teenage friends who
in old
Snapshots look almost like generic little kids, so
Young, in our memory they were as potent as
gods, each
With his own divine attributes. Here's the Kind
One
Among the bullies, his body hairless and muscular
in the
Shower, a tiny mole on his left cheek, his blond
hair always carefully carded as we
Wrestle under the lilac bushes next to the church
where
His father is the minister or something; or here is
the tennis
Champ who lies in twin beds in the light with me
for hours in
Underpants whom I may amuse but must not
touch. A touch will

Make him disappear forever, like pronouncing
Lohengrin's name.
Well, not forever, but for a long painful year.
Then there's the guy
With plush, powdery skin, a big house, a square
Knight's face, whose name I've forgotten but
should be called
Luke, who would sometimes wrestle with me,
sometimes
Not, then the fellow who'd sit across from me at
the library
Table after gym class, always smelling of sweat
and that
Special fried dandelion smell of a redhead, always
holding my legs with
His in a vise, our faces betraying nothing—but
look, I
Meant to talk about girls too, but it's only boys
I remember half a century later.

Hustlers

I'VE HIRED MEN FOR SEX all my life. I started as a teen in Cincinnati, Ohio, where I worked a summer job for my father. His office was just three blocks from Fountain Square, which was the very center of the shabby old city. He had had a beautiful office in the *Cincinnati Enquirer* building, an art deco masterpiece on Vine Street with its shining brass elevator doors and two-tone marble floors, but by my time in the late fifties he'd moved to his own plain-Jane two-story building a ten-minute walk away.

I had a company car, a generic white Plymouth, to get to work from my father's house in the suburbs. He slept all day and worked at home all night, though he drove into town at dawn to leave instructions to his employees printed by hand in block letters on paper with the embossed heading *From the desk of E. V. White.*

Maybe I was paid thirty dollars a week, which left me after basics twenty dollars to buy two men, the men in their twenties who sold their bodies for ten dollars each. They were what we called "hillbillies" from across the Ohio River in Covington, Kentucky. Their accents and their cocks were thick. They didn't kiss, they didn't suck or fuck, all they did was pull out a hard dick from piss-stained jeans and sit there in the car on a deserted alley next to a windowless brick wall until they came in my mouth. Nor did they talk.

I suppose in their eyes we were all alike, though I was sixteen and they were twenty-five and most of their customers were married men in their sixties, but our paying to suck cock made us pansies, pervs, sickos, hermaphrodites (which they pronounced "morfrodites"), faggots, queers, glandular cases. . . . I doubt if they had a theory of what caused homosexuality. To them we were degenerates, scum, homos, and once we put a cock in our mouth, we were irredeemable. Nice enough, maybe (but who wants to stick around to find out?). It was agreed that if we ever saw them with their friends, with a girl, we wouldn't say hello. In the 1950s we could only be a subject of a "problem play" for educated people or, for teenage girls, a sniggering article in a fan magazine ("Is Tab's horse a stallion? No, she's a mare, naturally. Tab's no queer"). Mostly people didn't talk about it. No one "came out" except drag queens and the campy peroxided waiter at the diner. Their looks came out for them. That was the era when all men wore coats and ties and hats. They tipped their hats when they saw women or older people they knew. In elevators, if ladies were present, they held their hats in their hands out of automatic respect. Indoors they didn't wear hats except in stores. Women wore little crushed hats nestled into their "hairdos" and never took them off, not even in the theater or at a luncheon. Except when they got home. At home they might also wriggle out of their painful girdles. Girls didn't wear girdles unless they were fat. I remember the first girl I danced with who had a slimming girdle on under her evening dress. The men's ties were narrow and sober; they came with tiepins. Most men wore white handkerchiefs folded in peaks protruding from their vest pockets. They wore glasses—that was before contacts. They had long black stockings—showing a white calf when you crossed your legs was frowned on. Nails should be clean and pared, shoes shined. You could sit in an elevated chair, put your feet onto solid-brass supports, and someone would stoop over your shoes to shine them for a dime. I can remember the shoeshine men would talk to one another in an incomprehensible dialect, full of whispered indignation.

I mention all that to suggest the class difference between me and the hillbilly hustlers. They certainly didn't think of themselves as homos. Getting a blow job wasn't queer; girls and queers sucked men's cocks. You were marked by what you did, not whom you did it with.

Just a way to get some extra change to waste on a girl at a bar.

Sometimes if the hustler was handsome and had a nice body, I'd get a hotel room in a flophouse for five bucks. The desk clerk knew we wouldn't be up there more than an hour. The hustler's fee would go up to fifteen dollars for total nudity—well, not total since usually he would keep his dirty socks on. He would lie back with his hands behind his head and let me feast on him. No kissing, no embraces, no ass licking, maybe ball kissing, no nipple tweaking, just cock sucking, *his* cock, no attention to my cock. The most I could hope for was that he'd push my head down on his cock and give a little yelp of agonized pleasure when he came. Of course I paid before the act. After sex he'd usually bound up, get dressed in a flash, and take the rickety elevator down. I'd sit on the edge of the bed in the light coming through the window from the two neon-red letters, the T and the E of the HOTEL sign, that hadn't burned out. All very noir. The downtown streets were deserted except for the sex traffic swarming around Fountain Square and a few vagrants sorting through the refuse in the public garbage cans. The old crime films of the forties replayed on TV always fascinate me. That's my world—of cars as big as kitchens, of men in suits, of flashy blonde dames, of gangsters grinning evilly. Only the dialogue is snappier than in Cincinnati in 1956.

On either side of Fountain Square—with its large statues of bronze women holding up bronze shells from which water dripped lazily tier to tier—were movie theaters. The RKO Lyric on one side and the RKO Grand on the other. I went to one once by myself to see, of all things, Hitler and Eva Braun's home movies from Berchtesgaden, in which the benign Führer played with his dog, waved at the camera, and smiled at Eva. I sat by myself in the nearly deserted theater, but soon a middle-aged man sat beside me with a raincoat in his lap. He draped the coat over his lap and mine, rubbed his flexed calf against mine (unflexed), then reached down to stroke my calf with his hand, all safely under our lap robe. Then he began to grope me, though he fended off my hand when I tried to touch his erection. My eagerness to participate must have disgusted him, as if I wasn't the innocent kid I resembled, the uninitiated straight lad whose crotch he hoped to plunder. I was a teen, I didn't shave yet, I was hard but I wasn't afraid. Perhaps I was queer myself, like a fruit that looks nearly ripe but, when you bite into it, is mushy, spoiled.

Tennessee Williams didn't have sex until he was twenty-eight. Later, during the war years, he made out like a bandit, hauling two or three men a night off the streets or out of the bars to his room in the Manhattan Sixty-third Street Y or the Hotel St. George in Brooklyn. Occasionally he was beat up (a violent trick was called dirt in the gay lingo of the period). The ideal of that time was not necessarily another gay man (though there were plenty of them) but rather a straight man who wanted to be serviced (*trade* in the gay language of the day—sometimes *straight trade*).

Naturally, making propositions to drunk straight sailors or truck drivers could be dangerous. On January 14, 1940, Williams writes in his diary:

> Probably the most shocking experience I've ever had with another human being when my trade turned "dirt." No physical violence resulted, but I was insulted, threatened, bullied, and robbed—of about $1.50 and a cigarette lighter. All my papers were rooted through and the pitiless, horrifying intimidation was carried on for about an hour. I was powerless. I could not ask for help. There was only me and him, a big guy. Well, I kept my head and I did not get panicky at any point though I expected certainly to be beaten. I didn't even tremble. I talked gently and reasonably in answer to all the horrible abuse. Somehow the very helplessness and apparent hopelessness of the situation prevented much fright. I stayed in the room while he was threatening and searching, because my mss. were there and I feared he might try to confiscate and destroy them. In that event I would have fought, called for help, anything! He finally despaired of finding any portable property of value and left, with the threat that any time he saw me he would kill me. I felt sick and disgusted. I think that this is the end of my traffic with such

> characters. Oh, I want to get away from here and lead a clean, simple, antiseptic life. . . .

So much is contained in this passage. The self-hatred and the quest for "real" men often put gays into the hands of blackmailers or brutes. The powerlessness was very real since at that time the police would never have protected a gay man; homosexuality was a worse crime than robbery or assault and battery (homosexuality was still a capital offense in some states). Finally, the increased disgust with oneself and a pledge to "reform" after being attacked was typical; the victim blamed himself. The individual note that Williams brings to this scenario is his fierce protectiveness toward his manuscripts if not to his own person. Also idiosyncratic is the use of elegant Southern turns of phrase ("portable property of value").

At one point a gay friend of Williams's announces,"We ought to be exterminated . . . for the good of society." Williams argues that gays are some of the most sensitive, humanitarian members of society, but his friend declares flatly, "We ought to be exterminated at the age of twenty-five."

* * *

I HAD OCCASIONAL GAY SEX with gay men and boys, but one reason I hired hustlers at such a young age was that I couldn't find many other gays. I was horny, I was fearless, I wasn't religious or even conventional, so I had no "moral" hang-ups. Which isn't to say I didn't feel shame and guilt. I pleaded with my father to send me to a psychiatrist so I could get "well" (my father reluctantly acceded). I'm afraid that a generalized amnesia has blotted out most of those painful memories (a terrible thing for a writer to confess). In my published memories I'm much more spunky and determined than I really was. Why didn't I become an alcoholic? Flunk out? Cut myself? I was an A student. My Texas mother had always said I was "sweet," even "wise" (other Southern middle-class boys will recognize the moral blackmail of the "sweet" designation).

I did contemplate suicide, though my intense, sobbing sessions could scarcely be described as "contemplation." I knew something was seriously wrong with me, that I was abnormal. I toyed with the idea that I was superior, as many gays once did. A bookish boy, I could reel off the names of putative gay geniuses in history. Those delusions of grandeur alternated with the most searing self-contempt, of abjection. I was a sissy, a freak, afraid in the outfield that the ball would come my way. I saw my life as emblematic, and in my sickest moments I suspected it was being constantly filmed, even when I slept.

Once I picked up a Fountain Square hustler who knew a specific place for me to park my car. Minutes later his "colleague" opened a door, caught me and his partner in flagrante delicto, brandished a knife, and ordered me to hand over my cash, watch, and high school class ring.

I begged him to let me keep my ring and he acquiesced (maybe he recognized it had no resale value).

I met a strapping guy on the highway who was hitchhiking to Cincinnati. I sped past him but doubled back to pick him up. He was friendly and I suggested I could get him a hotel room at one of my usual dumps. He was eager. Once in the room we both threw off our clothes. He made a muscle designed to excite me. What I was zeroing in on was his erection; within seconds I had it in my mouth and was contentedly sucking it like a nursling.

In those days I didn't care about the size of a cock. Only in college when I began to hang out with a "size queen" ("The really big ones can be detected as mounds running down on one side of the crotch") did I become alerted to that particular masculine attraction. When I first started hiring hustlers, I thought only of sucking cock, any cock; I would jerk off later thinking about it, about the whole forbidden transaction. As a seven-year-old I had stolen cigarettes and smoked them in the basement; I needed to be transgressive, though everyone thought of me as a sweet good boy. I had to recognize my own lawlessness while appearing to others as a solid citizen, president of the United Nations club, and leader of the glee club (at the YMCA I'd belonged to the Eisenhower Club).

After my hitchhiker shot his semen into my mouth, he became extra friendly and invited me to go on the road with him. I wasn't enthusiastic about that suggestion and told him I had a nice life at home and plenty of debutante parties to attend. My cold refusal infuriated him and he started choking me and ordered me to give him my expensive shoes. "But I can't. I can't walk down the street and go home past the maid in my stocking feet." I gave him some cash and, completely sullen and disgusted, he finally let me go. He didn't even want me to take the time to lace up my shoes but made me hobble off right away. He stayed in the room for the night, I suppose.

⋆ ⋆ ⋆

I MET A GAY MAN ten years older than me who was very camp—I'd never known this world of talking and joking. I learned expressions like "She dropped some beads . . . ," (which meant *he* hinted that he was gay), or "She has pencil meat" (the penis was small), or "He's rough trade" (meaning he wanted only to be sucked—and he might beat you up). I found out that the right way to refer to each other was as Miss Thing and to classify other gays as rice queens (liking Asians), dinge queens (liking Black people), chicken (adolescent men), and chicken hawks (older predators). We routinely called each other Mary.

My older gay friend encouraged me to hire hustlers and bring them into a deserted downtown church where he was the night watchman. He wanted me to suck them in the basement toilet while he watched from a dark room on the other side of an air shaft and open window. I ran into him maybe ten years later and he said he'd never known another such bold, fearless tot as me. He told me other gay boys were much shyer until they were in their twenties. Why had I been so brazen, so weird?

* * *

I HAVE A FRIEND WHO thinks sucking cock is a purely cerebral pleasure. There may be some erotism associated with the lips (are they why we enjoy kissing?) but there are no such receptors in the throat. The mouth is not a vagina nor an anus. But then what is the erotic charge in giving head?

I suppose it's sexy to kneel in front of a man, to look up at him as a child would. To know one is bringing him pleasure with practiced expertise is a delight. Since the word *cocksucker* is so charged, such a taboo, there is a pleasure in diving into the forbidden. In the fag's competition with women, it's exciting to turn the mouth (or ass) into a vagina. The reward of cum brings a Pavlovian satisfaction. Few gay men like sixty-nining; it's too confusing. We prefer to play one role or the other, the stud or the slut. A good cocksucker can produce whole wells of saliva, doesn't scrape the dick with teeth, can deep-throat, uses his hand as a gripping extension of his warm mouth, turns the hand to enhance penile pleasure. If he's a real pro, he warms his mouth with hot water first. He awakens the whole groin by licking the balls and the taint. He might have to finger a jaded man's asshole or bite his nipples if those have become the major erotic zones, as they often do with age. Many gay men are bored by their own dicks, dislike being sucked, and prefer anal fucking or to be fucked. A college friend, a painter with a low voice and a long cock, taught me how to suck cock. In those days we didn't have pornographic movies to imitate. We needed an actual instructor.

Years ago, I remember reading the findings of a therapist that many of his patients had masochistic fantasies if not practices. When he explored, he found out almost everyone fantasized about domination or submission, even heterosexual men and women, though few wanted to act on those fantasies. Could cock sucking be a dramatic, thrilling expression of submission to another man? The soundtrack that often accompanies cock sucking:

Him: "Take it all! Deeper, much deeper! That's it, gag on it."

You: "Oh, thank you, sir, for letting me suck this big, hard dick, a real man's cock, it's so hard, I can't take it all. You're going to hold my head between your hands and fuck my face? Oh, I want that hot cum all over my face!"

So many men are used to masturbation that they like to take over just before they cum, as though they consider an orgasm a private matter. Of course in pornographic films the men also jerk off when they climax—the "money shot," which would not be visible in someone's mouth or ass. The rhythm, the syncopation, the depth of plunging, the degree of moisture, the level of concentration on the middle eye, the speed and urgency, even the verbal cues ("I'm cumming! I'm cumming! Oh, God . . .")—these are all idiosyncratic and remind you that most people invented rather than imitated their style of wanking. Whereas their fucking style was patterned on their first partner's, their early-adolescent adventures in masturbation were solitary. Maybe that's why masturbation was considered a sin by priests—it replaces the tribal function of sex with the solitary ecstasies of onanism. Maybe that's why some men have to fuck their pillow to cum or have to turn their hand thumb down—all learned behavior learned alone.

In the seventies, between Stonewall and AIDS, everything changed. Now young gay medical students or publishing interns began to advertise in the *Village Voice* or the alternative papers such as the *East Village Eye* or the *Advocate*. There would be their name (invented), their stats, their rate per hour, their phone number. These guys just needed money for (as the French say) their "ends of the month." Since I was still in my thirties, went to the gym, smoked marijuana, I was probably a surprisingly easy client. These guys kissed, told their stories, knew from the phone call what you expected.

I even hustled myself once. Why not? An older gay friend called me and asked if I wanted to "do a double" with him. We showed up to a shabby hotel room and found two chubby businessmen with hair on their shoulders dressed in white underpants. They were sweating and smelled of BO. After our fun and games, they played electronic versions of classical music, some enormity called *Switched-On Bach.* My friend had told me to play dumb and I did. I kept trying to guess who or what Bach was, and the businessmen would explain, all the while rolling their eyes and laughing. They liked dumb, I gave them dumb.

For my own hustlers, I used a "madam," a gay man with a gay voice who'd smoked too many Kools, someone who had a whole stable on call. You'd say over the phone, "I want a tall blond top in his twenties for around two in the morning." He'd say, "Hold on, doll," and on another phone he'd call two or three matches or close matches to my description and check on their availability. Then he'd get back on with me and say, "André is available. He's a six-foot top with eleven inches, uncircumcised, thirty-inch waist, volunteer fireman, hairless, will wear his uniform if you so desire. He'll be there for one hundred dollars at two A.M., cash. And tipping is encouraged. Uniform or not?"

"Not. Thanks."

I ordered up someone at that hour to make myself stay in and work on my remunerative freelance writing. I was always ghostwriting textbooks (U.S. history was my specialty) or about the lives of the composers to go with sets of records; to this day I know surprisingly detailed things about Brahms, Mendelssohn, Handel, and

Copland. The most exciting thing was buzzing my trick in and hearing his footsteps on the wooden stairs. Then the Reveal: I'd open the door and he'd come in, a little pudgier and paler and older than by expensive porno standards, but nevertheless better than I could do on the open market. Soon we were kissing (he tasted of cigarettes and Clorets) and he had pushed a hand down my jeans and was obligingly fingering my butt.

After sex he'd confess he wasn't really a fireman but a flute student at the Mannes School of Music and I'd joke about his embouchure and brag that I was a wannabe novelist.

Soon after "André" had come in the door, he'd phone in to the madam right away to show that he'd arrived safely and the setup was kosher. I'd slip him the *petit cadeau* immediately. Then we made passionate love that seemed more voluntary than commercial, more an impulse than a transaction. He put a yard of tongue down my mouth and a yard of penis up my hole. We grappled and sweated and moaned. As he and I were lying around afterward stewing in our own juices, he said, "Was that as good as I think it was?"

"Hell yeah."

He chewed his cud for a while and said, "That was amazing!"

"I thought so, too."

"I was wondering if you'd go out with me on a date?"

"Sure."

"For free," he specified.

"Groovy," I said (that was the period).

He took me to a midtown dance club that would exist for only a year. He slipped me a pill and soon I was staggering and jiggling and groping him. Finally after an evening on the dance floor that seemed as long as *Das Rheingold*, we grabbed a taxi and sped off through the deserted streets to his fifth-floor railroad apartment. He had a big dog that wanted to go out as much as we wanted to fuck. André (who was really named Earl) did take him out for a quick walk, which made me like him more—kind to animals. When he came back, we devoured each other.

"I wish I could get to the country with my dog," he said. "If I could get away and play with him in the country, I'd get off speed and start living a healthy life. Now when I'm not out on a call or walking Horatio, I'm speeding and beading with my friend Josie."

"What? Speeding and . . ."

"Beading. Josie lives upstairs and she's a speed freak, too, and she comes down and we listen to the Ramones and do lots of beading. We've covered hundreds of throw pillows and at least ten pairs of jeans and two denim jackets with colored beads."

"Do you sell them?"

"No, it's just something to do. My mother gave me her old gold-thread drapes and I liked the thread but not the drapes, so one night while I was speeding, I picked all the thread apart and wound it around spools and then set it up on a pint-sized loom I have and made a very simple jumpsuit out of it and did it all in one long forty-eight-hour session, wanna see? It's kinda sexy, especially in the crotch."

He went into the bathroom and changed. When he came out, I said, "Hubba-hubba," or something dumb, though dress-up did nothing for me and as a wannabe writer I could imagine spending that many hours only on a paragraph or two. The idea of killing time seemed a melancholy pursuit. He was sexy in the jumpsuit, especially the way it stretched across his narrow butt, though it did look obviously homemade. "What did Josie make?"

"Huh?"

"While you were unpicking the curtains and weaving your jumpsuit?"

"Oh, she just comes and goes because she lives upstairs, did I say that? She's in the life, too, but the guys come to her. I'm too paranoid to have my johns rolling up here, I don't know why, I couldn't tell you why. But recently, I think, she's been beading pillowcases."

I asked him if he really wanted to take his dog to the country. Would that really help him get off drugs?

"Drugs? That's so bogue, man."

"Isn't speed like a kind of drug?"

"I guess you think pot is a drug!"

"I'm really naïve," I said, though I was the least naïve person alive.

It took him a moment to calm down and become less surly. I told him I had a girlfriend who had a house in the Hamptons we could borrow for a few days. I could rent a car and Earl and Horatio his collie, could come out with me for three or four days. Would he like that? I knew he was a vegetarian and we could stock the fridge with healthy vegetables. He laughed and said, "Vegetarians like desserts and bread more than vegetables. We're not vegans." (I had never heard the word *vegan* before. The other new word was *macrobiotic*.) Earl got a faraway look in his eyes and even shed some tears.

"You're saving my life. I can't wait to be in the country and to play with the dog." He scratched Horatio's white belly (the dog was on his caramel back) and said in baby talk, "Horatio, the nice man is going to take us to the country and help us get healthy again and play and play!"

I rented a car and drove us to my friend's lovely house in the Hamptons. Earl retreated instantly into the room I'd given him and my only contact with him during our three-day stay was the glimpse of his pale, startled face I'd see when he opened the door to eat the food I'd brought up to him. I had to walk the dog.

* * *

AS THE YEARS went by and I got older, I became a more typical client. The internet arrived with its lists of "masseurs" on Craigslist. The hustlers were still rather high-end: office workers, grade school teachers, out-of-work actors who preferred hustling to waiting. I knew a hustler who said he had to cum five times a day and it was hard to round up that many free tricks on the street or in bars; only prostitution fulfilled his needs. Everyone for free took too long to cozy up and break the ice, even in the leather bars. We used to say *S&M* stood for "stand and model." The approach in normal bars was too slow. The slightest smile or acknowledgment was taken as a come-on. One talked only to an actual friend. That was the magic of backroom bars. In a silent dark room the direct approach was the only move possible. Whereas in a hustler bar (in the Theater District or on Second Avenue in the Fifties) everyone had an excuse for talking; people were either buying or selling. There is nothing more animated than a hustler bar.

I began to treat men in general as if they were pay-to-play. On the internet I would exchange emails with normal guys who were too young or hung for me to get; I would type out ordinary letter$ with dollar $igns. To a hot young literary man, straight, someone I knew in Philadelphia, I offered two hundred dollars and he said, "Sure." It was never repeated but it felt like a bond over the years, at least to me. I had seen his beautiful muscular body. Is that what I wanted? Universal availability? In the early eighties I would hire countless men in a Cretan village. It was paradise. Everyone was available for a price, even the mayor. To the moralistic American friends who worried about the "power imbalance" of such exchanges,

I'd say, Would you rather live in a world where every man was available for a slight sum, or in one where only the usual 5 percent of the population was gay and haveable?

I fell in love with several hustlers as I entered my sixties and seventies. One of them, a tall Mormon blond, was the man I had sex with more times than with anyone else in my life. We traveled to Edinburgh for the festival and to Greece. He charged me every time we had sex, hundreds of times. He was a poet–rap artist and would organize readings but never acknowledge me in public. I guess I was too old to plausibly be a friend of his. His brother, I heard, had a blond Mohawk and would roam the dorms of Brigham Young University, looking for girls to seduce in short order. His father was a bishop in the church but also a crystal meth dealer and addict. My friend used meth, fought it for years on end, kept relapsing. He moved to San Francisco, found a young lover, appeared in local productions of musicals. We exchanged hundreds of emails, mostly practical, but many of them endearing.

Then one day he was dead. His lover emailed me. He'd started using again and the electrolytes had been stripped out of his body or something. He'd been trudging up a hill in the Mission District when he suddenly fell. I invited the lover out to New York. He was a nice guy. We reminisced. He cried. I cried.

⋆ ⋆ ⋆

WHAT DO I THINK OF sixty years of hiring men for sex?

First, if you pay for it, you can get someone cuter than your usual conquest.

Second, it's efficient. They arrive when you want, leave when you like, no wasted hours cruising.

Third, they'll do what you want within limits Since 90 percent of gay men (at least in New York) are bottoms, you're safer hiring someone who agrees to impersonate a top from the outset.

Fourth, if you have a *gout exclusif* for Nordic blonds or hairless Asians or athletic African Americans, you can get one, even when they're not numerous on the ground. If you like young but legal, you're in luck.

Fifth, if you're ashamed of your body, now you have something to offer instead: money.

Sixth, the whole transaction can be sexy. The john need not disguise his admiration, the hustler need not hide his preening.

* * *

AGAINST ALL THESE PLUSES, THERE are several minuses. It's a fairly expensive hobby. There's a power imbalance, but it's not clear exactly how it functions. The john seems to have control, to be the director commanding the actors, but the minute they step out of their roles and go out into the real world, the john is ignored and everyone cruises the hustler, because he's the handsome one. If in their "scene" together the john calls the shots, often the john arranges for the hustler to dominate him. It's a transaction but no more so than that between employer-employee, rich husband–dependent wife, professor-student, though the dyad john-hustler is more transparent, cleaner, more straightforward, more consensual.

The greatest disadvantage is that respectable people, including respectable gays, disapprove.

That's also the greatest advantage.

Stan

MY FIRST HUSBAND WAS STAN. I saw him at college starring in an adaptation of Rilke's *The Notebooks of Malte Laurids Brigge*, playing Malte of course. With blond highlights. The play was a plotless mystic mess, perfect for the twenty-two-year-old I was. Stan had a concentrated, soft-spoken way of acting, as if he'd forgotten to wear his contacts.

I was so taken by his beauty, his perfect old-fashioned John Barrymore looks (which earned Barrymore the cam name The Profile), that I invited the whole twenty-two-member cast back to my house for an opening-night party. Everyone came except Stan. I mixed drinks with the pure alcohol one of my housemates got from his chemistry lab—and fruit juice or Coke. The next day the house was full of guests who'd passed out but were still alive. Stan, befitting his romantic role, had gone alone for a long poetic walk in the arboretum.

Luckily I knew the playwright, whom we had ungraciously dubbed Graybelly because of his coloring and waist size. "So you like our little Stan, do you? Join the crowd. But be warned: *She's* a little bitch. All she wants is to destroy men." Reluctantly he gave me Stan's details, who turned out not to have an iota of the bitch about him; he was more the bewildered ingenue.

I went to Stan's address and rang his buzzer. He didn't ask who it was, just buzzed me in. He lived on the ground floor. He looked surprised, but not too surprised, when he saw me (problems with his contacts again?). He was shorter than he'd looked onstage but even more beautiful with his classical nose, which soared without a bump out of his forehead, his luxurious golden hair, his penetrating blue eyes echoed by the color of his sweater, carefully selected no doubt. He smiled in a general way as a movie star looks over the crowd. His complexion was faultless and glowing, as if a light were shining through the best Belgian linen.

I told him that he had been brilliant last night, that I was a fan and had missed him at the cast party (and I thought, I'll do anything at all to stay in your presence, please, please, for the rest of my life). He knew how to "play" modesty, but I couldn't imagine how I'd respond any better than he did to praise from a stranger. He asked me if I wanted a cup of instant coffee. I said, "Sure." I supervised the process as if he needed my help.

I had never had a lover and the whole concept was new. If you could get another young man to go with you, you'd be half of a couple, at least in the eyes of the six or seven other gay men who knew you were out and didn't think it was a neurotic sham. As someone kind and intelligent and honest, you might be able to seduce someone above your pay grade. A beauty might be willing to team up with a devoted nerd; wasn't that the whole point of Woody Allen movies? Under the right circumstances the Beast, if kissed by Belle, might turn into a prince. What the Beast had to offer was eternal, royal devotion.

Answering my questions, Stan said he was from Lansing, Michigan, from an old Scottish family who had emigrated to Canada and eventually to the States. His mother was a heavy-drinking gossip columnist for the local paper from a family of Anglican ministers, he explained. His father had become a self-made millionaire (like my father) by supplying industry with machinery. Stan had four brothers; he was the second oldest. Neither of us used the word *millionaire*.

His parents gave Stan a tiny allowance on the very American principle that poverty was character building; Stan worked shelving books at the library for a dollar an hour. Studying, working, and rehearsing filled his days. He hadn't realized he was handsome or gay until a dorm roommate attempted suicide when Stan didn't return his interest (actually, Stan told me, he was attracted to the guy but afraid to show it). Stan might have suspected his own orientation; he had watched cowboy-and-Indian movies on TV from age twelve since the Indians were the only men of that period who were bare chested. Much later he took up with a Puerto Rican lover who reminded him of those early crushes.

He didn't ask me questions. I only asked him because asking personal questions in the Midwest wasn't considered rude but a sign of interest. I told him I'd be coming to the play every night. He looked flattered-embarrassed. His new roommate let himself in, a drawling man with bad hair, drooping eyelids, and gold jewelry. I was extremely cordial to him; I've always known to court the wife or friend. He seemed responsive to the attention. Later Stan told me Leon's chauffeur had driven him all the way out from New York with just one overnight stop. When they arrived, Leon didn't invite the chauffeur in after he'd delivered all the matching luggage but just said, "Okay, Mitch, you can go now."

I went backstage after my second evening at the theater; Stan looked confused because so many new friends, mostly gay men, had flocked to his dressing room. He wasn't used to having so many admirers. The play wasn't good and Stan wasn't very good, either. He was too "inner," as they say in acting class; his performance was like that of a firefly toward the end of its luminescence, pulsing more and more feebly in your hand.

I was obsessed with him, not sexually but religiously. It never occurred to me to do anything sexual with him except kissing. Or just to look at him. One night when I was prowling next to his ground-floor apartment, I found a window open and climbed into his bedroom. He was asleep. I stared at him, his pale face on a paler pillow, until he awakened and sat up and said politely, "Who are you? I don't have my contacts in."

When I said my name, I wasn't sure he remembered it. But when he put it together, that I'd climbed through his window like a passionate lover, he became friendlier. His beauty drove men mad and he liked proof of it. Once, a year later when he was living in New York, a flustered famous clothes designer screeched to a halt on Christopher Street in a royal-blue Mercedes and invited Stan, a complete stranger to him, to Egypt; Stan politely declined. He had his job as a copyboy at Time Life and had already used up all his vacation days (two weeks). Stan lived cautiously.

His family was unusual. His uncle shot his wife dead then killed himself. Stan's father took his mother on a Caribbean cruise. When they returned to East Lansing, he sent her off to the pharmacy to pick something up. He phoned her there and told her not to come home but to call the police. Naturally she hurried home and discovered her husband's head on one side of the room and his body on the other. On a later occasion she drank so much she didn't notice that she'd left her car door wide open and reversed next to a tree, wrenching the door backward into the front fender. She had then driven home and parked in the front yard and gotten out without saying anything to anyone in the house. The only entertainment she'd submit to in New York was the ballet, which had three intermissions for refills. Two of Stan's brothers killed themselves. The mother would die a natural death, if cirrhosis is considered natural. She thought of herself as fun loving and gay in the old sense; she resented homosexuals for spoiling that enchanting word. Under her breath she routinely whispered to no purpose the slogan of a once-popular jazz musician: "You're hearing George Shearing." She often enjoined the male members of her family to "lighten up."

I flew to New York with just $250 in my pocket on July 19, Stan's twentieth birthday. I sat on the doorstep of the building where he was staying with the star of *The Fantasticks*; I was supposed to be a wonderful surprise. He never came home that night. I checked into the West Side YMCA, where Tennessee Williams purportedly swam every day; it wasn't air-conditioned and if I left my door open for a little breeze, I'd wake up to see someone in a towel in my doorway clawing at his crotch; I hadn't promised (ever, to anyone) to be faithful, but I was in love, which at the beginning equals fidelity. No one else interested me.

Stan had one more year at college, but once he'd had a bite of the Big Apple, he couldn't accept any other nourishment. After a two months' search and a big loan I'd found a rent-controlled apartment and a job; Stan had worn out his welcome with the *Fantasticks* star, who preferred Nordic brutes to passive Greek gods. I got Stan a job as a copyboy at *Time* and with no other options he moved in with me.

We slept on a foldout couch left by Sandy, the woman from whom we were subletting. We had sex only three times; my specialty was other bottoms, with whom I was compatible socially and psychologically but not sexually. Bottoms are nicer and more interesting, sweeter and kinder. They're a disappointment only in the sack. Tops are mean and aggressive, until they turn into bottoms. (A guy online advertises as "the only top in New York.")

Stan was the god of anxiety and depression, if that deity is deceptively handsome and seemingly serene. He was depressed daily, not so surprising given his family history and, probably, genetic burden. He had a tiny wardrobe but it could take hours of changing these few clothes before he was ready to go out for a burger at the local coffee shop or a drop-off at the Chinese laundry.

We were both young and adventurous; I was cute enough (though only old snapshots suggest that that might have been true) and he was an immortal beauty. In that pre-AIDS era our worst enemies were crabs and (for bottoms) clap in the ass. I remember once picking up on Greenwich Avenue a man famous, as I later discovered, for writing a long-running musical. After sex he said, "You've got the same *carry-on* as this guy I fucked last night, Stan something, sort of hysterical and refined like you." He was Tom Eyen, who wrote the lyrics and book for *Dreamgirls*. That came later, in 1981; when we knew him, Tom was writing dozens of off-off hits such as *Why Hanna's Skirt Won't Stay Down* and Bette Midler's first show. He was the most prolific camp of his day, the star of Caffe Cino and La MaMa, someone racing to write his entire oeuvre as if forewarned he'd die from AIDS at fifty.

Stan wanted to be an actor and attended the Herbert Berghof school of acting. Our tiny apartment was always full of girls smoking, wearing black tights, and speaking in fascinating, smoke-damaged voices. Scene study was what they were up to, with time out for aspirational talk about their "career objectives," giggling, half-whispered accounts of gallant adventures, and well-rehearsed complaints about their parents. If they were Catholic, they would also tell horror stories about nuns. Stan appeared in plays at Caffe Cino, including some by Lanford Wilson, who was then so poor he'd share our starchy dinners. It was a place where the owner, Joe Cino, would stand by the espresso machine, and eventually killed himself, where off-off-Broadway was born and the Warhol crowd hung out and sometimes acted.

Stan was usually depressed, sighing and fighting his devils. He would wake up screaming, sometimes after being approached in his sleep by a determined murderer with a knife—sad, resigned, but one who looked just like him. His double was a handsome murderer with an uninterruptible if resigned will of his own, a comely golem. Stan knew, sort of, that he was a famous beauty, watched his weight, and would stay home if he had even a tiny blister on his lip. He had a strange malady; if you wrote something on his back, it would come up as red letters on white skin—dermatographia. It could be a clue in a mystery if the dying victim wrote the name of his killer on someone's back; the graph usually vanished after thirty minutes, so the detective would have to be quick! It was caused by stress, caffeine, and hot showers. I took it as another sign of Stan's mythical origins as a god.

We met a well-known Mexican photographer who lived on the whole top floor of the Rhinelander Castle (72nd and Madison) and drove a Bugatti; he took big, black-and-white portraits of Stan. They would go on road trips to nearby sylvan or marine destinations. Edgar was his own stylist, flattening Stan's shirt collar or loosening a hyacinthine curl on a brow more marmoreal than manly.

I wrote a play and put Stan in it. The play didn't make much sense—it wanted to be "experimental" but echoed Ionesco's already stale devices—though at least it earned Stan his Equity card before it closed in a month on a hot night in May. Years later I met the English critic who'd written in *Theater Arts* that it was one of the two best plays of that season. He had absolutely no memory of it. The star was the Black actress Cicely Tyson, the first person ever to tell me about poppers. Somewhere in print she recalled the play as something comically confusing.

I'd drag men home when I knew Stan was working. I remember a big Southerner who fucked me as I wiggled my butt to show passion, though he kept saying in his baritone drawl, "Just lay still, little honey." More wiggling and he'd say, "C'mon, baby, just lay still for me." I thought his bad grammar proved he was a lifelong top. I was surprised he was turned on by an inert bottom.

Stan thought it would be humiliating if people found out he was in my play and living with me, so for a few weeks he moved out to a boardinghouse on Twelfth Street right off Fifth Avenue. In those days the West Village was still bohemian in the sense of *La bohème*; Stan's new best friend at the boardinghouse was a handsome guy named Mario, crippled, who made artificial flowers and sold them on the street, someone right out of Puccini, sweet with waves of black hair, smiley, a modulated, deep speaking voice, a bit mysterious (where was he from? How had he learned to make crepe-paper blossoms? Did he have a sex life? How old was he?).

After the play closed, Stan was willing to move back in with me. We were too much alike to have sex but one night while I was asleep beside him, he fucked me; as I slowly rose to consciousness, I realized, for the first time, I actually liked being screwed—physically, I mean, not just theatrically. So much of gay sex and love (all sex? All love?) is verbal, coded fantasies of possession or submission, pocket dramas of eternal love, parting, or reconciliation, of projection or triangulation, of love at first sight or, as in the Bing Crosby standard, written by Sammy Cahn and composed by Jimmy Van Heusen:

> Love is lovelier the second time around,
> Just as wonderful with both feet on the ground.

In my cynical view, love the second time around is a statistical rarity, more a consoling aspiration than a reality. We shouldn't complain of our Hollywood or Top Ten versions of romance. Unlike the troubadours, at least we have a chance of feeling up the Beloved or dancing with the person in Paris or in the rain, whereas those men, who invented love, could only praise and serve Her, the boss's wife, a remote, rather ball-shrinking stand-in for the Virgin Mary.

Stan was always nice, never angry, unfailingly polite, generous. But depressed. And confused as to why he was depressed. He couldn't talk his way into insights because his depression blinded him, like the hood placed on the prisoner facing the firing squad. He was so absorbed by his insecurities that he couldn't really follow a conversation; if he did catch a joke he would laugh woodenly, a beat too late, more a Bitcoin of humor than solid-gold mirth.

Being from rich households, as Stan and I were, meant that we thought of money only enough to pay the rent and the electric bill. I bought an off-the-rack suit from Hardy Amies (the Queen's couturier) on five payments of twenty dollars. We counted out our pennies to see if we had ninety-eight cents each to go to the ballet and sit in the top balcony of the City Center, home to the Mecca Shriners (where you could at least see the dancers' feet, which was impossible from the first rows of the orchestra). We experimented with lunch at a Zen restaurant where the vinegary vegetables were arranged mysteriously by principles of yang and yin. At a large restaurant nearby called Larre's you could eat a cup of lentil soup, say, sweetbreads in black butter, and a wobbly pudding for three dollars. That was our usual lunch spot. We saw the beginnings of pop art in the Fifty-seventh Street galleries—all during our lunch hour or hours. George Segal's cast-from-life white plaster sculptures might be seen stretching to change the black letters spelling out the name of the new movie on a dimly lit theater marquee, or large pictures of Warhol's Campbell's soups cans might be lined against one wall, or we might chuckle over Lichtenstein's comics ("Vick! I—I thought I heard a voice . . ."). At first we imagined they might be satirical but then we read that Warhol said pop was a way of liking things, and we reoriented our orreries.

Given his family background, Stan needed to see a therapist. He resented paying someone to listen to him. I tried to reason with him, to point out that a therapist was a professional, probably with vast student loans and sizable Manhattan rents, that friends were the free ones and never listened since they were too busy matching anecdotes or exaggerating their own raw deals (rawer, rawest) or their ordeals with nuns. We paid people to listen, to bite their lips, not to talk about the clerics who ruined their childhood.

Stan and I went our separate ways though we continued to live together. We went to San Juan for a cheap winter holiday and stayed in the YMCA on the edge of the old city where the buses turned around. Every morning after *café con leche* we'd take the #10 bus to Condado Beach, where we'd swim and sit under the towering hotels until they blocked the sun in the afternoon with their sheer bulk. We became friendly with two locals who were impossibly old, in their midthirties, but in good shape with teakwood tans, excellent English, and muscled chests. They led us to a deserted underfurnished apartment two blocks inland, where they fucked us in the same room on twin beds without sheets while laughing and chatting with each other in Spanish in which an occasional word in English would surface like a goldfish breaking through murky, algae-streaked water ("tight," "pretty," "ass"). They came at the same moment with a shout of triumph and hurried us along through the front door, our butts full of cum and our sneakers unlaced. We stumbled back across the fields of weeds through which tiny lizards darted. The half-dug ditches stank of sewage. When we finally found our towels on the beach, they looked sad but blameless, little rags we'd brought with us on the plane from New York. I shit out my partner's semen (which we called his "babies"). I was pleased to see how copious it/they were. It wasn't part of our intimacy repertoire for me to ask Stan how much sperm he'd harvested.

In Puerto Rico I'd picked up a husky, undemonstrative guy my age named Jesus, and Stan had found a more refined, lighter-skinned young man named Pepito, very reserved, who was proud to belong to the Castilian Club, restricted, I gathered, to those who could trace their roots back to Spanish colonists. They came to visit us in New York and—sadly for Stan—on landing, Pepito became Pepita! Very feminine in gaudy clothes. My Jesus remained stoic and masculine, proudly Taíno. Once when we got on a bus in San Juan, an old man started sneezing in a stagy way. I asked Jesus why and he explained that in Puerto Rico a gay was called a duck (*pato*) and our feathers were getting in the man's nose.

San Juan had several gay bars in the old city, where the streets were cobbled with blue stones used as ballast in sailing ships in the eighteenth century. A gay bar would typically be on a side street. Customers were inspected at a gate on the ground floor and would go up worn stone steps to a dim, high-ceilinged room with overhead fans. We'd dance the salsa and sip rum-and-pineapple drinks. After midnight the narrow streets were empty except in the *calle* that led up to the prison, where the confined men would howl and play with themselves whenever they caught sight of a few ducks. Brown-skinned construction workers on scaffolding would make a similar fuss when we gays would swish past. Unaccompanied gringo genetic females would elicit even louder wolf whistles and sucking sounds.

Of course, like most gay men we were uninformed about heterosexuality and just dismissed it as what "squares" did. Imagine our surprise when on our next trip we stayed in a beautiful bed-and-breakfast right next to the governor's palace. We shared the spacious eighteenth-century space (the kitchen, the sitting room) with a pimp and his tattooed whore. They also dealt drugs. I think their prey were rich gringo tourists in the nearby luxury hotel El Convento, built as a convent in 1646, or some of the island bureaucrats hovering around this brightly painted, fully restored historic district. I say "uninformed" because we didn't understand why they were always sweating, never tan, up all night, calling out jovially as clients arrived and departed. Of course, we were up all night, too, dancing and cruising into the cool recesses of daybreak.

I say "uninformed" because in Paris in the eighties I knew a gay man from Cleveland and his Asian lover who bought a little house at the back of a noble garden. The man didn't understand why his house had eight bedrooms with eight bathrooms outfitted with bidets and no kitchen, why it had secret passages from the entrance to the bedrooms; then we discovered that it was a high-class bordello from the early twentieth century. Gays, who imagine they understand the mechanics of society because they sleep with men of different social classes, often fail to see the intriguing straight life rustling around them. I remember a straight sex publication of the eighties, *Screw*, wrote that the cities I identified as gay meccas in *States of Desire: Travels in Gay America* were also the only cities in our big, sad country with any real straight action.

* * *

EVEN THOUGH STAN WAS ONLY a copyboy in New York, the Newspaper Guild was such a strong union that his employer, *Time* magazine, paid his tuition to New York University, where he returned to finish his first degree and then an MA in English. He studied with Leon Edel, Henry James's tireless, five-volume biographer. Someone told us Edel even wore James's underpants! And Edel retired to Honolulu, where I couldn't quite picture James with his coconut, ukulele, and lei. And skivvies. Edel was a Freudian. I sat in on his lecture on *The Bostonians*, one of my favorites; Edel dismissed it, doubtless because it was lesbian, and Freud, the sterling literary critic, thought of homosexuality as "a kind of failure."

We moved to a big apartment on West Seventy-first Street. Later I learned the neighborhood was called Needle Park because of its reputation as a center for heroin addicts. As I was coming home late one night, I saw a man in a hat and overcoat shoot another man similarly outfitted; the victim fell to the sidewalk and a woman shouted and sank to her knees to embrace the body. Since Kennedy men rarely wore hats, that stood out as much as the violence. The next morning I told Stan I'd seen someone with a hat murdered on our block. Only the hat seemed to draw a hint of surprise. We just shrugged. We'd become real New Yorkers.

I was seeing a shrink, who was trying to cure me of homosexuality, though she saw my sex life as nothing more than a symptom of a deeper disorder. When in all seriousness I told my best girlfriend, Marilyn (who was lesbian), that I needed to stop "acting out," she went pale but said in a normal conversational tone, "I don't think we can still be friends. When I met you, you had a fine mind, but now you've ruined it by being brainwashed by this pseudoscience."

I was shocked but knew she was wrong. I'd spent years studying Freud and even interpreted the dreams of chums at the office. Everything was sex, and sex was childhood. Luckily I didn't lose her friendship; I just avoided certain topics. And over the years I became as skeptical as she was about Freud. I thought the first tentative step toward heterosexuality would be to move out and away from

Stan. I broke the bad news to him, which I thought he'd take in stride. I was surprised by his forlorn expression, since we'd led separate lives for most of the eight years we'd known each other. A popular song at the time (1967) was the Four Tops' "Seven Rooms of Gloom," which Stan was always humming or singing in those final days. I thought of my new chic little apartment on Thirteenth Street in the West Village as a temple to my newfound or about-to-be-found heterosexuality.

Soon enough I was lonely and horny, two conditions so frequently coupled that it might be called *lorny*, which sounds better to my ear than *honely*, maybe because I think it's related to *forlorn*, the saddest word in the language. (I assert this with all the confidence of Edgar Allan Poe, who declared the most beautiful phrase in English was *cellar door.* In my mind I gallicize it as *Célidore*, some sort of Molière heroine).

Those were the days of street cruising or bar cruising. No dating sites, no chat lines, no back rooms, just seduction on the hoof (sometimes an orgy in the back of a parked truck or in the crumbling piers on the Hudson).

I wanted to be pure, to stop acting out, to court a nice girl—to reinvent myself entirely. New York was big enough and anonymous enough to be able to do a complete makeover. New friends. New, lower voice with fewer swooping intonations, less hissing, fewer interrogatives, more statements, less dentition, more blurring. A fascinating older woman at work, a linguist, had a theory that gay boys sought refuge with—and identified with—public school teachers, especially librarians. These women, according to my colleague, had aristocratic pretensions but working-class salaries and demonstrated their social aspirations by over-articulating (they were, as her theory went, the ultimate source of the gay voice). I never met anyone else who agreed with this theory, though I've tried it out on many language experts.

Out of loneliness I dragged so many men home, some for a month, most for a night. Stan found a nice apartment on the mysterious intersection of West Fourth and West Tenth and outfitted it with a small, prodigiously hung Nuyorican twenty-year-old named José, a smart scholarship student at NYU, a smiling, patient little guy who saw everything with his big, comprehending eyes—and who practiced salsa moves every afternoon with another Latino in Stan's living room. I'd always just assumed Latin teens were born to twist and turn, to suddenly reverse direction, to move on oiled haunches, to look bored in a carefully engineered spin; it was a revelation now to watch them rehearse, to talk it over in Spanglish, to work out new combinations, to count, to stop suddenly in frustration, sigh, mumble, then go back to practice. Smooth as puree, hot as chili pepper.

Stan had a velleity toward bad boys and violent men. Though he was so proper, held up as the ultimate WASP by his thuggish admirers, he craved living on the Wild Side. I never knew if his taste for louche characters led him to drugs or if getting high was his real goal, easier to accept if some beloved tyrant was ordering him to smoke it, swallow it, shoot it up. He fell in with a powerful Aldo Ray double ("You're one of the most wanted men in America," the blonde says before kissing Aldo), an ex-marine with a shot-up right arm, a gravelly, gruff voice, someone with a good, wide-eyed sincerity act, the determination of a pulp hero swimming under ice toward freedom—and the best drugs in town. We all met him in our lithe, clean-shaven late twenties at Riis Park, a beach you could reach by public transportation, a bleak stretch of sand named after a social reformer, a place turned into a riot in June by drag queens emerging out of hastily raised tents, lip-synching Dionne Warwick, their eye shadow impeccable over stuffed bras and suppressed genitalia in gaudy bikinis. In the midst of these miracle plays, which started with the Fall of Lucifer and ended with the Last Judgment (your job to envision the drag equivalents to these dramas), this hairy, overweight man (wearing a diplomatic sash of raw flesh where he'd just been operated on for shrapnel) was talking in his sanded-down Aldo Ray, breathy tenor about his exploits in 'Nam, the day he saved his whole squadron when the gooks trapped them in the deepest, wettest jungle. We were gay boys who'd never had even a schoolyard tussle, who'd claimed we had "homosexual tendencies" to avoid the draft, who ran past American war movies in favor of Swedish existential explorations. We felt daring if we smoked a hand-rolled marijuana cigarette though more often we came home reeling drunk on vodka tonics.

The little queens I was with were not impressed by the war stories and the guy's obvious urgency about impressing us with his heroism and near-death escapes. They wanted to comment on the latest hits out of Motown, fashion trends, and hair-straightening techniques; they couldn't be bothered by this military blowhard, and when he went off to buy a hot dog, we moved our towels away. Little did I realize this comical marine would become a part of my life for the next twenty years.

What happened was that Stan met him at a bar, fell in love with him, became a drug addict, missed so many days of work he was fired. His beautiful face and body were used as bright bait for luring guys into orgies. Jeremy (or the Goon as I named him) found them all an apartment at the foot of Christopher Street overflowing with greasy wrappers from ordered-in fast food, jockstraps dangling from the shower curtain rod, pink plastic bongs over a reservoir of water, the smell of poppers and vomit, a room full of a couch in many sections, a shag rug with cigarette holes burned into it, an empty fridge with just a frosty jar of pickles and a Coke can laboring under Pleistocene layers of ice. A toaster oven that no longer worked; a roasted fly was sitting on top of it like a symbol. They tried to make me a part of their life, but I wasn't hot enough, fun enough. I drove with them in their powerful Chrysler station wagon to Killington, Vermont, and a rented chalet where they all skied and had an orgy before plunging back to New York for the post–Black Party orgy. I went with them to Fire Island Pines and the Octagon house they were renting; they played their music so loud all night that the neighbors petitioned to have them banned from the island. Banned from Fire Island—that must have been a first! I got so high from something the Goon concocted for us that I was soon crawling across the floor to lick the golden legs of a buzz-cut DJ in shorts. I was burning up with desire. The DJ was polite but uninterested, really an embarrassed monument to indifference. He moved so little, seemed such an object, that I had to stroke him to make sure he was warm and alive. One Easter we all crashed into a midnight mass, smelling of sniffed ether and bourbon; the Goon, who claimed to be Russian Orthodox, kept making the sign of the cross with two horizontal bars. We kept shushing each other and left en masse halfway through the homily.

Ultimately, though, I was too square and couldn't keep up. The Goon kept all his studs ecstatic and obedient through sleep deprivation, meager meals, and copious lashings of drugs and booze. I was so uninitiated I couldn't identify what we were swallowing—three letters, I remember, in an ever-evolving exploration of the alphabet. If someone couldn't sleep, it would be four 10 mg Ambiens; if he couldn't take the whole fist, two quaaludes. Everything else seemed to be a horse tranquilizer. MDMA, mephedrone, various opioids, barbiturates, ketamine, meperidine (for childbirth, normally)—all of these mixed in an appealing cocktail, often with cranberry juice and ice.

Stan told me that after one of those weekends he came to (or rather became conscious again though he had been walking and talking on automatic, apparently) in a diner on Sheridan Square. Sitting over a plate of ham and sunny-side up eggs that looked up at him like two jaundiced eyes. He had no idea how he'd gotten there. He asked the waiter what day it was. Tuesday, he was told. He realized he hadn't gone to work in over a week and a half. After another year of that and a major convulsion that ended him up in the hospital, he moved in with me on Eighty-sixth and Columbus. It was a huge apartment with many windows. When we stopped answering the Goon's telephone calls, he set up a machine gun at our level on the other side of the street on a rooftop. Stan pitied him and went back to him though he'd promised he never would. He was also in some sort of drug withdrawal.

His life was saved by Alcoholics Anonymous, where he is still an active member fifty years later. He and another guy escaped from the Goon's cult and they're still together decades later. The Goon himself ended up in a veterans' old age home in California. The one time Stan visited him he staggered behind Stan's rented car until the attendants pulled him back to his room. He was pleading with Stan to come back, to "save" him.

Stan became a solid, sober citizen, spiritual, funny, who had a long, honorable career in publishing. But his real passion was in helping people—young, old, rich, poor, male, female—fight addiction. And he is still volunteering at eighty-two.

Keith

THROUGHOUT THE 1970S I was in love with Keith McDermott, ten years younger than me. When I first met him, I was living in a third-floor walk-up studio on Horatio Street in the West Village. He was living across the street with Larry Kert (he's dead), the original young male lead in *West Side Story.* I was one of Larry's rainy-day fucks—he'd call me midday or early evening when he was horny and the weather forbade open-air cruising (snow, rain, or tropical heat). Maybe I met Keith at Larry's or through someone else; I don't remember. Keith was living rent-free with Larry. They'd started out as lovers but now, after a year, Keith was expected to help in maintaining their big, luxurious apartment by cleaning and doing chores—and disappearing when Larry had a trick he was bringing home.

Keith wanted to move and I had a lead on an eight-room prewar apartment on the Upper West Side, a block away from Central Park and just four hundred dollars a month. The landlady lived downstairs from us and had decided to rent only to gays—but, what narrowed the field, gay men without dogs. In those days gay couples had dogs, not yet children. We were too poor and unsettled to think of wanting a dog. It never crossed our minds.

Keith was a famous beauty (famous in the West Village and Fire Island among gay men). He was blond, blue-eyed, just twenty-one, and perfectly formed (an expert gymnast). In good weather he rode his bike everywhere. The sound of the whirring wheels as he came racing around the corner and glided to a halt became the very whisper of desire for me. He was fleet, funny, and so handsome that Bruce Weber, the most famous photographer of handsome men back then (Abercrombie & Fitch, *GQ*, Calvin Klein), took his picture. Weber's men, often nude or in wet white underpants, were twentysomething, athletic, Ivy League, and passably heterosexual—perfect eye candy for gay men of the period, who liked their men to be iconic and unobtainable, i.e. straight.

Of course I wanted to sleep with this beauty, but he found a way to forestall my lust. He said he was sick of "meaningless" sex and invited me to join his chastity club. We could sleep side by side as long as we never touched. I was content to have that constant access to his beauty and company—and he was happy, I guess, to reap the devotion of a fit, charming, bewitched man in his early thirties who was just publishing his first novel. Before long we were living in our vast eight-room apartment. Whenever I would buy an ugly but big dining room table and six high-backed chairs at Goodwill, Keith would be so outraged that he would drag the furniture out the front door into the hallway. He was a resolute artist and had a horror of looking or being middle-class.

Keith was careful with his "instrument," i.e., his body. He drank tiny cups of liquid buffalo grass, ate sparingly, mainly vegetables, and visited the gym daily for two hours, where he'd twist and turn on the exercise rings, climb ropes, and strengthen his arms and core, his shoulders and legs, but he never wanted to become a heavily built muscleman. He was a Peter Pan, the *puer aeternus*. I was abject in my longing for him. I can't bear to recall the scenes of my crawling toward him, arms outstretched, or the moment when I saw him as an emanation of God. Once I organized an orgy of several guys I dragged back from the Candle Bar in the neighborhood, hoping to be able to touch Keith in the melee. It worked.

Larry Kert had had a cruel streak—maybe that had rubbed off on Keith. Or maybe my idolatry was just that absurd and I needed vinegar poured in my wounds. I suppose some of the mystical strains in *Nocturnes for the King of Naples*, the book I was writing then, were a spillover from my almost religious love for Keith.

And then Keith was cast in the Broadway hit *Equus*, in which he was naked onstage eight performances a week for years. Dirty old men would sit with binoculars in the front row night after night. A pimple on his ass would send Keith into an anxiety attack. He was brilliant in the role; I saw him in the play dozens of times opposite Richard Burton or Anthony Perkins. It was such a titanic strain (no colds, no hemorrhoids, no weight gain or perceptible loss), thousands of lines, gymnastic feats blinding the "horses" (dancers dressed as stylized horses), rowdy adolescents seated in the cheap seats onstage making wisecracks, kids who were so used to TV that they thought these performers, too, couldn't hear their remarks. His life became one of iron discipline. I like to think he even came to appreciate our domestic life.

He moved to Los Angeles but was a little too openly, rebelliously gay for Hollywood in those days (no one wanted to see the fag kiss the girl and there were almost no gay roles in the seventies). Then I moved to Paris for sixteen years. When I came back to New York in the late nineties, Keith was living with a sweet, talented Israeli painter; he'd mellowed, was just as funny as ever, became a close associate of the avant-garde director Robert Wilson. Keith himself directed plays at La MaMa and had published a book. We're great friends. He insists that I helped form some of his tastes in music and literature. His own curiosity and experience in so many domains of the arts, however, didn't need my influence, I'm sure. When I told him I'd be writing about him in my sex memoir, he said, "Just say I have a big dick." That's easy—his dick is huge.

Pedro

I CAN'T PROCEED ENTIRELY CHRONOLOGICALLY, since desire does not obey any timetable. When we masturbate (at least when I do—or did, I'm too old for it now), we flash from one memory to another, skipping decades, in pursuit of excitement, not narrative sequence.

Maybe eighteen years ago (or ten) I first met Pedro online, on SilverDaddies, a dating site for "mature men and their admirers." He lived in Madrid, was in his early thirties, had a vacation coming up, wouldn't mind visiting New York. I offered to pay half his airfare and, of course, put him up.

He took the train in from the airport in Newark, and as he came up the stairs at Penn Station, I instantly recognized him: young, slender, glossy black hair as if he'd been dipped in tar, happy but shy. We walked the nine blocks to my place and I could see his English would be a problem until we got in bed. He kept frowning every time I asked him something, as if he were hard of hearing instead of uncomprehending. Almost as if he were offended. His vowels were hollow as if he were speaking through a long drainpipe.

We made love five times in a row, or rather he fucked me five times and I jerked off twice. Then we posed for cell phone photos, our mouths bright red with ambient color from wild kisses, my expression smug as a conquistador's and his sheepish, his face almost defeated in victory.

He told me he worked in computers for the Madrid subway, that he was from a provincial coastal town, that his father (who'd disappeared) was Spanish and his mother from Ecuador. He looked indigenously Ecuadorian with his hairless body, dark nipples, glossy pubic thatch, humble and rounded shoulders, flat nose, wide lips, small dark eyes. He was white, but not ghost white like me; a drop of purple had toned down the gleam. It seemed he was ashamed of the Ecuador connection, and he explained several times that his mother had come over to Spain as a university student and had nothing to do with the later wave of peasant Ecuadorian immigrants—a distinction wasted on me.

He napped for hours, jet-lagged. When he woke up, I served him a big paella I'd made in his honor, which he didn't like; he hated fish. Later I made him one of his favorite dishes—an oily, potato-driven thing with sausage.

He was a courageous if inept speaker of English, though with enough consultations of the Spanish–English dictionary and enough lip-reading kisses, we communicated. He never wanted to go out and was as lazy as I, but it was a different kind of laziness, dark-circles-under-the-eyes weariness, a state one felt could be repaired with the addition of just one essential mineral. He seemed always exhausted, if stoic, his loins wrapped in a towel; I was like an old fat cat dozing beside the fire, only occasionally tempted to walk the three paces necessary to lap up another bowl of cream.

He liked to take long showers. He confessed he wanted to be tied up and blindfolded and sucked; I had enough matériel to oblige. I took pictures of him with my phone, all trussed up as he was; in the photos his penis looked red and raw though always erect.

I handed him half his airfare in cash—that had been our arrangement. I took him to see a revival of *Hair* on the theory that a musical wouldn't tax his English. We were both bored—and I, at least, was also repelled by the tacky reminders of the 1960s, which I'd lived through as if it had been a glorious epoch of youth culture and liberation. Now we saw it was all just misguided rhetoric, bad haircuts, and fake velvet and near-fur. We left our two-hundred-dollar seats at the intermission and returned home. I was fucked two more times that evening. I felt a bit like an opportunistic vampire.

I asked Pedro if he had any secret desires. He blushed and said he'd like to suck my cock. I was shocked and disappointed to see my god become a suppliant. I'd been willing to tie him up but not to submit to fellatio. I didn't like it. Did that make me a freak? Was I afraid of losing control? Of being impotent?

Once when I was in my twenties, after a man sucked me off, he said, "That's the only time in my life a guy came through a soft cock." I was always on the lookout to discover a man wasn't a real man, that he liked his tits pinched or asshole thumbed, that he would go soft unless you mauled his nipples, that he flirted automatically with any unshaved, thick-necked brute, or that he'd stare at you with imploring eyes if you stuck your fingers in his mouth or hole. For me, sex was mostly mental, an act of submission, even of humiliation, certainly not a proof of virility or a simple physical release. I could stay interested in sucking cock even immediately after I came. It was all theatrics, especially if my partner talked dirty. Friendliness and laughing, though welcome in off-duty moments, were cold water to a beast in heat. Sex was no laughing matter; domination especially had to be served without chuckles or smiles. Since we were all convinced that another gay man could only be *impersonating* virility, our partners had to pretend at least to be angry and unfeeling. Spelled out like that, the whole transaction sounds ridiculous, but I'm trying to approximate in words our unconscious scenarios. Mind you, plenty of men were Nice Guys all the way, but their smiles and kisses and gentleness were somehow less exciting than tit torture, spit and a sneer, painful sudden anal intrusions, biting, slapping, nasty insults: that was the true language of the great godlet Eros.

Pedro had a delicate, shame-faced manner, as if he'd just broken an expensive goblet and was tiptoeing away from the shards. But during sex he was rapacious, his wet, sharp-toothed mouth as wide as a shark's, his penis never wilting, his buttocks round and rubbery with youth, his eyes sleepy or blinking and startled if I said something in my treacherous, incomprehensible English.

And his desire for my poor old wreck of a body (I was seventy) was deeply consoling. I could tell I excited him. Online I'd learned he went for men who were "gordo, viejo, y passivo" (essentially, "fat old bottoms"). It was such a relief to have these qualities be not a source of shame but singled out as virtues I could flaunt.

I decided to spend two summer months in Madrid with him. I found a big, underfurnished apartment on sabbaticalhomes.com; the guy must have skipped town because bill collectors called every day. I think he was an American with a Spanish wife, children, and mother-in-law and a failing language school, or so I gathered from a video he'd left behind, which showed boisterous and numerous ugly people chattering in Spanish and serving each other big plates of food.

I soon came down with a bad case of agoraphobia and felt faint the instant I stepped out of my big apartment, which looked as if some creditor had sacked it. All day long I would clean the apartment, to little effect, cross the street to take money out of the cash machine, and lurk under the arcades to scuttle into the chicken shop, where the friendly butcher cut up a chicken into tiny pieces devoid of anatomical sense, into the sweets shop, where I could point to pastry and lacquered fruit pies, to the baker, for bread, and finally to the fruit-and-vegetable market. Because I was such a good customer, the clerks forgave my shyness and linguistic flaws.

Home to start parboiling and washing and setting the table. I never felt so much like a housewife, so lonely, so erased, so drugged on sex, or so inefficient. I'd forgotten I was a writer or professor; if I was a professor, it was like the one in *The Blue Angel*, who crows like a rooster for Marlene Dietrich.

I'd douche out my ass to get ready for Pedro's return. He'd come in about four, tired and sweaty; we'd sit on the strangely shaped, overstuffed couch and watch television, usually a variety show that would make Pedro smile with his pointed teeth, the shadow of a mustache over his full upper lip; sometimes he'd chuckle with his odd laugh like heavy coins rattling in a dry wooden church collection box. I never understood a word of the rapid, presumably clever dialogue; I couldn't even translate the title, which had the word *hiciste* in it, which I think is a form of the verb *hacer*, "to do" or "to make." Stunned by the language, my general incompetence, and by my advanced age, I prayed that my pussy wasn't leaking into my trousers.

We decided it was exciting to call my ass my "pussy." There's something so low, so dirty and humiliating, about that word if applied to a man, something so smelly and endocrinal, so soppy with animal secretions, that it repulses and shames at the same time. I have no idea whether *coño* has the same impact in Spanish, but after a few drinks Pedro liked pussy and cunt talk. It felt a bit less abjectly menstrual in another language. Maybe he could see how much it excited me.

We'd watch TV and then at a certain point (I could never predict when) he'd nudge me crudely and we'd go to the bedroom. We'd pull off our clothes and we'd stretch out on the bed; beside it on the wall were inserted "artistic" fragments of mirror. Pedro would study his reflection. I would suck him for a while and I wondered how my white hair looked against his glossy black pubic hairs—a sort of stark, puzzling Japanese woodcut.

Then he'd mount me, his juicy mouth biting my ear, his dick in my pussy, his eyes on the mirror.

Sometimes he'd seem disgusted with me, with my insatiable need for cock, though I never made a move or said a word even if I always seemed grateful for the attention. His certainty that I was voracious reminded me of the nineteenth-century male fantasy of the devouring woman who destroyed man. She was a lioness licking her paws, presenting her inflamed cunt to the poor, bewildered males, despoiling them of their family and fortune by revealing a glimpse of the hairy clam under whitecaps of lace. Her bed an altar to demeaning, insatiable lust—a huge silver Sicilian raft decorated with pairs of lovebirds and blinded cupids, but capable of witnessing a young man destroy his ambitions, fortune, and health, the length of his shaft sunk into the greedy, putrescent origin of the world, bubbling sulphurously amid the overgrown underbrush.

Pedro, though always exhausted, wanted to go out every night to the chubby-chaser club in Madrid's mile-square gay section, Chueca. There we'd stand in the corner. I learned to speak to no one and keep my eyes lowered like a Japanese bride lest I inadvertently lure a Spanish chaser to my side and provoke Pedro's rage. If I talked to a stranger, Pedro would later march the streets in silence, his jaw as solid as Gibraltar, and once home he'd drunkenly break dishes and throw furniture, sputtering with his broken English. It would end up with my sobbing, his tenderly but clumsily comforting me, as if he were a chimp trying to repair a delicate broken watch. Then he would brutally fuck me, his earlier anger reawakened with each thrust until he'd explode once again into this Venus flytrap between my legs.

Every day my Spanish teacher, Juan, would show up. Pedro was solicitous toward Juan, a younger, nonsexual friend whom Pedro had met in an old-fashioned café in Chueca, a spacious place with white plaster scrolls on the smoke-stained walls and an upstairs, like a Paris café. Juan was in his twenties. Permanently depressed, kind, effeminate, his perfume smelling like a urinal cake. As best I could tell, his depression was linked to his cocaine habit. His English was so much better than my Spanish, we usually just chatted in English about his "anguish."

Pedro, I realized, was starved for friends, and that's why he adored Juan. Pedro had his extraordinary sexual gift, but it could be shared only with old chubbies. He desperately wanted to be a chaser among chasers, but he was always having his invitations to all the young, slender chasers of the Chueca fat clubs turned down; they didn't want to go to the movies or go out cruising with him. He wasn't nineteen or handsome, nor did he have a prestigious job, and he looked suspiciously . . . Indian. I who had been a published writer for thirty years had nearly forgotten how hard it was to make friends when I was a nobody; as a youngster I liked anyone who liked me. In the past I was like him, always being blown off. No wonder he treasured his friendship with Juan, who admired him and truly needed him.

Juan was so fragile psychologically that he lived at home with his parents, though he owned a large, newly painted and furnished apartment that just sat empty until he got better. Pedro and I went with him on a pilgrimage to Juan's apartment, all gleaming and spotless in a remote, undistinguished neighborhood. On the walls were posters for Broadway musicals, as far from his real experience as New York, which he'd never visited—unreal entertainments in an unreal apartment, complete with two bathrooms and a kitchen with all the modern conveniences.

If Juan was dull with his nagging but nameless problems, Pedro's ex, a man of my age named Diego, was funny and seasoned, a well-known film critic who spoke several languages and lived in a cavernous apartment hung with good paintings and outfitted with a dinner table for twenty. And in a historic neighborhood. He was wry and warm, as if every rough surface had been ground down with travel and drink and sex and endless deadlines. Whereas with Juan our strained Berlitz conversations often stalemated, Diego could discuss anything approximately in any language—he was my kind of guy and my esteem for Pedro (and myself) went up; if he had had Diego as a lover, then he could attract anyone.

Whereas Juan's apartment was delivered right out of an IKEA catalog, Diego's was dog-eared with books and glowing with lamps wearing ruby shawls instead of ecru shades. There were stacks of newspapers and magazines in which he had articles. On the walls were photos of his new Japanese lover, a sleek martial arts brute who chose to live in the Pyrenees and rarely visit Madrid.

Pedro and I went once to the movies and once to a flamenco performance and once to a literary party on a balcony, but most of our evenings were devoted to the two main chubby-chaser bars in Chueca. Smoking was still permitted at that time; giant ceiling fans sucked the smoke out of the air. The music was pounding, popular and Spanish. Since I don't drink and could not benefit from the time-warping powers of alcohol, every second crept slowly by. The chubbies interested me not at all, and I was forbidden to look at the chasers.

One night Pedro must've thought I was too friendly to another chub; he didn't talk to me as we sped in a taxi through the avenues past buildings that looked as if they'd been designed by a confectioner rather than an architect. At home he poured himself another Scotch and began throwing plates and chairs around. Did it excite him seeing me cringe, my hands above my head for protection, or when I closed myself behind a door, whimpering? When I opened the door finally, he looked abashed and pulled me with his big hand, terra-cotta still cooling from the kiln, into the bedroom, where he covered me with devouring kisses and shoved four fingers up my hole, then put his hand in my mouth, giving me a taste of my own medicine. Whom did he learn all these things from, I wondered, sophisticated acts meant to look primitive? He held on to me tight that night as if he were afraid of losing me. And he nearly had.

Every day my goal was to get to the nearby Prado, though as soon as I was outdoors, I felt as vulnerable as a lobster without a shell, a little lightheaded, even stymied. I'd become such a Madrid housewife, elderly but cooking, cleaning, douching, trying to please a somber husband, my ass in the air, victim to his alcoholic rages, a mail-order bride not young or pretty, forced to smile painfully through riotous TV comedies I couldn't understand before offering up my rump once again.

One day I hailed a cab on the corner and took it to the Prado, though it was only on the other side of the park. Once I was inside, I became my New York self again and I steered myself through the Velázquez and Goya paintings, evaluating, thinking of clever things to say about the collection, once again an epicure with high standards and wide aesthetic experience, a New York exquisite, not just an Iberian drudge with a pair of warm holes.

We were going to go to Paris for the weekend but at the gate I discovered I'd lost my passport (or it had been pickpocketed) and we slunk home, defeated. Then began weeks of visits to the American embassy to procure a new passport, finally based on a personal interview with the Spanish employee of the embassy. Did he think I looked authentically, innocently American? I had lost my identity. But at last I obtained the document.

Then we went to Rome, where we stayed with an Italian diplomat friend, who combined an energetic social verve with an austere Hinduism (he'd been stationed for years in India). He had a whole Sri Lankan family living in the maid's room off the kitchen, though when we let ourselves into the apartment unexpectedly, we discovered a diapered brown baby or two on the kitchen floor. Everything was spotless and sumptuous in his prewar Parioli apartment with its gaudy screens of the odd Vishnu or angry Kali and its big windows overlooking the gardens belonging to a Mussolini grandchild.

We'd do the obligatory bits of tourism and snap photos of each other in the Colosseum or in front of St. Peter's. Pedro wanted me to buy him shirts and sweaters printed with asymmetrical abstract designs in strange colors, aubergine and pale iodine yellow. I imagined him wearing them in the smoky Madrid chubby-chaser bars.

We slept in one of the two living rooms on a foldout couch, where Pedro fucked me so hard that we splintered the mattress frame; when I looked at his face, it was as cold and inaccessible as a Central American god's, Chacmool's (a reclining figure, head turned to one side, on his lap a bowl for human blood). I was (and am) such a middle-class twerp that all I could worry about was the damage we'd caused.

Then came the day our host gave a party in "my" honor—dozens of facelifted Italian matrons in silk dresses cooing over me (they'd been instructed I was an important writer, though no one had heard of me). Some French queens were there, too, who'd known a countess who'd dropped me years ago and I had to pretend I was up-to-date on her and her son's brilliant marriage to a princess. There was much simpering and guffawing and every time I tried to slip away to check on Pedro another Italian lady would start her small talk. Once you fall into the glue trap of an Italian conversation, there's no escaping.

At last I discovered that Pedro had locked himself into our host's bedroom. I begged him to open up but he refused. One of the two bathrooms was in that room and I could see how exasperated the host was, especially since he'd outfitted that bathroom with all the fluffy, sweet-smelling, delicious niceties an Italian contessa might require to wipe her ass. When Pedro finally unlocked the door, his face was red and streaked with tears. He sobbed on my shoulder. He was wearing one of his asymmetrically printed sweaters I'd paid nineteen euros for.

"But what happened? Did someone say something mean to you?"

"I don't belong here. I can't speak Italian and no one understands my English. This is your world, all these writers and countesses! What am I supposed to say to them? 'Hi, I'm Pedro, I work in the Madrid subway'? . . . 'Yes, I fuck Mr. White.' "

I started to say, "Oh, Pedro, don't be ridiculous, don't underestimate yourself, you have a very interesting life, you have plenty to talk about," but I couldn't think of a single thing that would interest anyone here. Even the elegant queens, who might like to get fucked by him in a dark room—or anywhere else anonymous—wouldn't want to be seen with him, so devoid of beauty or pedigree or position or money, especially if they had to introduce him to one of their friends. In the world of the party everyone came with a short label ("He's a descendant of the Sufis," "She was short-listed for the Goncourt," "He's Gabriel's uncle, from the Lorraine Hapsburgs"). Pedro didn't have a label beyond being Spanish and living in Madrid.

"Everyone was laughing like animals."

"I know. They're horrible people."

"I heard you laughing," Pedro shouted. "You was laugh!"

And I'm sure I was, indefatigable little pleaser that I am.

Finally the last people drained away with many a merry declaration of "What a pleasure!" and "See you soon!"

Maybe it's coherent with my sexual masochism that I like telling stories that put me in a bad light. It's something I often do, act badly, but only in autofiction. In "real life" I'm kind and considerate, as I was with Pedro, as I still am with our Italian host, a generous, intelligent friend. Maybe writing itself needs to be written with a scalpel, not a brush. Or maybe I feel impregnable and honest only if I rush in to anticipate and say the worst possible things about myself that anyone could come up with. In my bleak Buddhist view, this concentration, even negative concentration on self, is just more egotism . . . Or literary daredevilry.

Pedro occasionally stays in touch. He's happy with a new elderly boyfriend, this time English. I suppose he'll be retiring soon.

Mini-Stories

THE THING ABOUT GAY LIFE is that you have countless mini-adventures, which years later leave only the faintest groove on your cortex. The handsome big blond with the sweetest smile and strongest Boston accent I'd ever heard, who wanted to get fucked only and moved out to San Diego, where he caught the eye of many a sailor, got infected with AIDS, and died.

The young Kennedy-style gay politician whom I invited to dinner after yet another bad affair on the principle that I should shoot high and aim for the top. He came to dinner more than once, we had "sophisticated" (i.e., cold) sex, and he got AIDS and died.

My French translator, a skinny boy with an enormous dick and fat lips and an encyclopedic knowledge of the French classics from Rabelais to Benjamin Constant called on me in New York and I immediately groped him—which he thought (rightfully) was disrespectful and unprofessional. I couldn't explain to him how every male in New York was fair game. He got AIDS and died.

Bruce Chatwin. Robert Mapplethorpe sent Bruce over to visit me and we were still standing in the doorway when we started groping each other. I saw him many times after that in London and Paris, but we never fooled around again. We had gotten that out of the way. Years later he contracted AIDS and died but couldn't accept that he had such a banal disease and claimed he'd contracted a rare malady in China from whale meat or something. Maybe the subterfuge was caused by his being married to a woman.

The dear friend of mine who knew I was not-so-secretly lusting after him and, one afternoon in Maine, in an exquisite house built by Buddhist monks after their abbot had disbanded them, came into my room after a shower wrapped in a towel and asked for a back rub. I gave him a blow job. That silent concession sealed our friendship and I never plagued him again. I wish I'd been that generous with older unattractive friends who lusted after me when I was young.

The doughy blond trick my age, thirty at the time, who spent the night gabbing with me after we had desultory sex. At dawn I said to him, "I'll bet you were raised a Christian Scientist, as I was." He asked me however I'd figured that out. "Because," I said, "you're such an optimist and don't seem to believe in evil. That's such a fundamental part of Mary Baker Eddy's beliefs—and her most unsettling error. Worse than her distrust of medicine."

* * *

I WAS RAPED TWO OR three times by clever older men, although we didn't call it rape then. Only later did I realize I'd been fucked against my will. One importunate man was an English television producer with whom I'd spent many a social evening in London and New York. He was the sort of stereotypical P. G. Wodehouse gentleman who'd suddenly stop in the middle of the sidewalk, let his eyes dramatically unfocus as if he were having an attack of aphasia, and actually say with perfect articulation, and a look of astonished disbelief, "What!?"

Maybe an Englishman would know how to reply, but I was disarmed, nonplussed. He invited himself up to my cockroach-infested, mold-in-the-coffee-cup studio apartment, despite my objections. I could dress myself presentably but my apartment revealed the depths of my poverty. Within seconds he'd wrestled me to the broken-back cot with the dirty sheets and peeled off my jeans and underpants and stuck his cock into my hole. He later told several mutual friends he'd never seen such abject squalor before. The next morning my rectum hurt, but I thought nothing more of it.

Another Englishman, a Cambridge don who was an authority on Arabic literature and who was visiting my university for a term, invited me to his apartment, got me drunk on martinis, and soon had my rump in the air, my legs bent back; after feasting on my hole he plunged into it and left me bleeding and unsatisfied on his bed. He put on his robe, washed away the blood and feces, went into the sitting room, made a cup of tea for himself, and took up a book. I pulled myself together and slunk away. For years afterward I bragged that I knew him.

There was a close friend of mine in London with an unheated apartment near Bond Street, in which I stayed in the 1960s countless times. In 1970, when I lived in Rome, John came to visit me for a few weeks. He was what I called in those days "a character." He hated the royal family with a passion. He seemed terribly repressed and proper, but when a lover told him while they were driving through Scotland that he was leaving him, John said in a clipped voice, "Very well," turned the wheel, and drove them off a cliff. They both spent the next year in full body casts. John had had his nose broken and remade several times but he was never quite satisfied with it. Every morning he'd make tea and listen to the "wireless" chat shows, including the *Woman's Hour.* He knew every bus route in London and even their late-night schedules. He was good at living on nothing a year; he made orange juice from powder in water. He ate something called cauliflower cheese. He said *ate* as *et.*

Everything in London was foreign starting with the fat, stubby key pushed into a low lock on the outer door—the "chub key." We would take the tube to Hampstead Heath, past the house where he said Rudolf Nureyev lived with his lover, Peter O'Toole (or was it Terence Stamp? Probably neither). We ran about among the trees and bushes on the heath, like the "mad things" we were. I wished my host, who was short and snug in his jeans and black leather jacket, wouldn't speak in such a deep, camp voice (he was a trained actor) and refer to me as "Miss Thing." We were just sliding out of the era of heavy-drinking Tallulah impersonators into the pot-smoking Village People period of the weight-lifting, hypermasculine clone. I lifted weights and John told me that was unhealthy and that later it would all turn to lard, which was true. The first time I saw a mustache in a gay bar I said to my cruising buddy, "Eeeww . . . I'd never kiss a man with a mustache, would you?" Six weeks later we both had them.

I would do anything, look any way, that would get me laid. I couldn't believe guys years later would advertise themselves by the boot brand or high-tops they wore. In France I remember men saying they were style *santiags* (cowboy boots) or *crade* (unwashed). Wasn't the body or even the personality under the look more important than the accessories? I would wear anything from a red hankie back-left pocket (aggressive penetrator) to yellow back-right (piss swallower) if I thought someone, anyone, would like that. I suppose I believed one's essence was enduring and unshod and of a neutral color and that accessories, so important to the poor and young, were immaterial,

I must have felt or been felt by hundreds of men on the Heath; I particularly liked deep soul kissing with a mustachioed stranger as the wind blew through our hair and the leaves above us shivered and the swift-moving clouds obscured the moon and stars. "Are you there, Miss Thing? Ready to go?" that bass, highly inflected voice would ask out of the darkness.

Daring myself, I asked the tall, slender, impossibly young man in my arms (he smelled of good soap) if he'd like to come home with us; our "flat" was on Marylebone High Street (which I'd learned to call "Marl-bun"). He said yes and my host, John, who resented snooty boys from Oxford and thought aristocrats should be beheaded, seemed a bit grim as we walked (downhill) all the way from Hampstead to Bond Street. Every hundred paces the Oxonian and I would stop a second to "snog," much to John's irritation, and the snooty trick never drew a breath and kept talking about the beauties of "Keys," which I finally understood was his college, Caius, at Cambridge. At last we were in bed and he was "good value" as a sexual partner, lithe, loving, versatile. In the morning I asked him if he wanted a "scone," which I pronounced as it was written.

He said, "I can't bear to think I shared a bed with someone who speaks like that."

"How should it be said?"

"*Skun.*"

★ ★ ★

A YOUNG, SLENDER REDHEAD, TALLER than me, came up to me at a trendy East Village café, the KGB Bar, which was on the second floor, up a long, perilous staircase, and said in a deep voice, "Mr. White, I'd like to interview you about intergenerational sex. Would that be possible?"

"You bet," I said, feeling like a starving dog at the door to a meat locker. It was 1985 and I was forty-five.

He was someone I would have been attracted to even in my first youth, when I was cute and picky. Well, to be honest, not so picky since I scored with someone every night.

We made a date at my place for dinner, one I prepared with loving care. My Paris trainer used to say if you give anyone enough wine and pass the poppers, you can get him. I guess I'm too romantic for thinking about seduction techniques. I try never to impose myself on someone who doesn't fancy older men (or let's just say the "old"). I taught for decades but never slept with a student (one ex-student on graduation day). I let the other person make the first move.

He was a fascinating dinner companion. He had an unusual self-assurance and smiled knowingly as if he'd already understood what you were saying. It was the early days of the internet and he told one story after another—stories he'd researched for *Plugged In* or some such trendy magazine. The story that struck me most was of an American who met an Englishwoman online. Through constant rambling and intimate conversations, they found they were perfectly suited to each other, fell in love, and decided to marry. He flew to London—and discovered she was sixty and he thirty. The age difference, which they'd never established during their hundreds of hours online, seemed insignificant next to all their shared values and expectations. They married and lived together happily back in his native Akron, to the astonishment of their friends and relatives, and both worked in the diner he owned. My date, Denver (not his real name) presented the internet as something spiritual, linking souls on the deepest level; of course we all know the cesspool of lying, vitriol, and unscrupulous subterfuge it eventually became, but in those pioneer years it promised to be a new, exciting utopia.

As if this scarcely believable story had been a preview of his own obliviousness of the barriers posed by age, he began to kiss me immediately after dinner. I'm lucky enough to have a functioning fireplace in Manhattan. I lit the logs I'd previously laid and soon we were naked on the floor beside the blaze. The thick red hair on his head and the sleeves of glinting red gold on his arms and the shield of pliant red on his chest and stomach, not to mention his burning bush, seemed too good to be true. We had memorable sex but afterward he complained I was somehow too experienced, too slutty, too quick and adept in assuming the position. He didn't like how I'd expertly swiveled my ass up to his waiting cock. What he wanted was a timid, gray, recently divorced, elderly man who would reluctantly give way to Denver's ardor—someone wooden and naïve, astonished by his own acquiescence, endowed with the purity of the until-recently heterosexual, the clumsy paterfamilias who'd shamefully nursed forbidden fantasies of a fiery young redhead, someone who would finally surrender to the redhead's passion but mutter later that that battering had really hurt, darn it. I felt I was being punished for not being a nerd.

I lost touch with him but discovered he was teaching in upstate New York and had become a sought-after screenwriter. From a movie magazine I learned where he was teaching. He'd also found a gray, tubby lover of a certain age. Denver brought the lover to a pizza party at my place. All the handsome, wasp-waisted, bumblebee-torso "boys," forty years old and well launched in their careers as writers, filmmakers, and designers, clever and expensively coiffed and shod, though the clothes in between head and feet were "young," generic, and off-the-rack—they were all buzzing around Denver with his red hair, low, resonant voice, growing fame, unimpeachable masculinity. They could scarcely believe they weren't his type and that balding guy alone in the corner was his chosen lover.

I found out that Denver's father was a chauffeur for a car service and had ferried Joyce Carol Oates and me to New York more than once. There we were, brightly chattering and oblivious in the back seat while Denver's father under his black hat with its badge and shiny bill drove us into the gathering February dusk. Little did we know this ideal young man had sprung from these quite ordinary loins.

⋆ ⋆ ⋆

THERE WAS THE GUY I met online who said he was a Scottish top. I asked him if he could wear a kilt while I bottomed for him. He lived in a worker's cottage in Brooklyn, only one room on each floor. It was a square brick building with an arts-and-crafts wooden door—a multipaneled oak door with clear-glass side lights. There was a fire in the fireplace, which had dusty blue tiles all around it.

The Scot was tall and slender and decked out in full regalia—a kilt, a short black jacket with silver buttons, high socks, a sort of pouch or purse on a chain around his waist, the sporran. I knew that under the plaid kilt there was a dick and hairy balls, no underpants. He was younger than forty and had a wide mouth full of white teeth, blue eyes as blue and large as a songbird's eggs if they were made of crystal, a sharp nose, and an accent that was almost intelligible, though less and less so as I became more and more stoned on the joints he was feeding me. He seemed surprised and slightly vexed that I hadn't brought any weed with me, as if I were just another freeloader bottom who expected to be kept high and well fucked. Which I was. Or so it seemed. He didn't say much. I was worried that I'd made a faux pas. He ordered me to take off my clothes and kneel. I obeyed.

I could see his erection ticking up and dimpling his kilt. I always became hypnotized by cock when I was stoned; my nipples ached in anticipation of their being worked. I was so insecure about my body that my very shame felt erotic—vulnerable, despicable if despising was on the program, worthy of being punished, *eager* to be punished. His mouth, now that it was closed in an unsmiling line, was exactly as long and straight as each eyebrow, a Morse code of male beauty or maybe like the oblong pitches in a medieval hymnal.

He snapped his fingers and pointed to the tip of his black slippers, not bedroom slippers but the kind you traditionally wear with a kilt. I crawled over there, as big and awkward as Mr. Snuffleupagus in *Sesame Street*, a muppet so large and unwieldy that it takes two people to operate him. The Scot, Robert was his name, sat on a high stool next to the fireplace and folded back the panels of his kilt to reveal his big erection as Christ tears open his chest to display his red, red Sacred Heart. I began to slide my pot-dry mouth up and down on the veined shaft. He kept up a muttered narrative with his incomprehensible accent; he might as well have been speaking

Plattdeutsch. Before long he had me in the room upstairs, his bedroom with its gigantic bed covered with a taut rubber sheet.

His older lover showed up and began to order me around in an accent I couldn't place. He tried to fist me and I said I wasn't quite ready for that. The idea excited me, but I'd never tried it. He said, "If I split you open, so what? Why do we all have this expensive health insurance if we never use it?" His accent sounded Slavic, which made it all the more sinister. I never did figure out his nationality. I thought his remark about health insurance sounded disagreeably fatalistic and bleak.

We had many rematches, the three of us. Once I was ordered to bring a young fourth for the Slavic lover (he wasn't really into old men). The guy I brought along was a handsome Mormon hustler/actor/poet/waiter; Robert and his lover suspected he was hired flesh and seemed to be against that in principle. I kept assuring them he was a friend, which he was, though in truth I did pay him—but they were dubious. The Slav sucked him and Robert fucked him, though he only liked to dominate the elderly and the overweight. I couldn't believe he didn't prefer this healthy, happy, brawny blond with the beautiful skin and glittering smile, his slim waist and big chest, his low voice and the movements of an athlete, graceful but not intentionally graceful.

Another evening Robert wore tight-fitting leathers and he and the Slav shaved my body. On yet another evening we all went to a restaurant in the neighborhood and Robert waited in the men's room for me to come in there and get fucked in a public place, but I was too stoned to understand what I was supposed to do. On another cold evening, he greeted me at the door to his house in a jockstrap and began to flog me. I bellowed my pain but both he and the Slav shushed me; they were afraid a neighbor passing by might hear my cries. They didn't want theirs to be known as the House of Pain. Then we all moved to the bathroom upstairs. The Slav and I crouched in the tub whereas Robert stood up on the sink and aimed his piss at one of us or the other. We both competed for it like seals begging for fish. I make it sound comical but it was as serious as a christening.

Then Robert broke up with the Slav, who'd become a serious drunk and fell down the stairs repeatedly. They sold their little house and the Slav moved back to Poland. Soon he was dead, I heard, from drink; maybe the breakup (or his retirement from his fascinating job) had destroyed him—or maybe he died just from the habitual progress of alcoholism (my AA friends and family members have taught me not to search for psychological reasons for alcoholism but to recognize it is not a symptom but the disease itself).

Robert became a loving nonsexual friend though I relished stories about his own exploits. He and his new lover went to a fisting colony in Normandy (it no longer exists) and there Robert pushed an entire football up a

Frenchman's rear; the man had to visit a local surgeon. Curiously, a whole queue of ass-hungry men were lined up before Robert's door at the colony the next day. They, too, wanted to be worthy of a serious operation. In Berlin when Robert ran into the man who'd needed surgery, that guy was ready for a rematch—greedy glutes!

Robert is always courtly now—to the point of actually reading my countless books! In his huge penthouse apartment that looks out on all four directions at Manhattan, he has parties, peopled with handsome young professionals and even a few women. Cute caterers are circulating with champagne and caviar. He couldn't be kinder or more respectful. He praises my prose to his nonreading, rich gay friends. I remember the first opera I saw as a child in New York. It was *The Magic Flute* at the Old Met. The hero had to pass through the frighteningly believable trials of fire and water to enter his father's temple; that seemed like what I'd gone through to bask in Robert's esteem (though secretly I was nostalgic for the trials).

* * *

WOMEN? YOU ASK. IN THE horrid old days we used to call them fag hags. The women who frequented gay men liked that they were around. The men tended to be good-looking, fun, muscular, always laughing, and good dancers. They went out almost every night, unlike their straight counterparts, who played only on weekends. Gay men could be flirtatious and (if you got them drunk and they were young) would even fuck you. Older ones or sober ones seemed more committed to their "lifestyle." Gay guys would sleep with you and snuggle, pretend to be a lady's boyfriend on an evening out with the boss or the visiting relatives from Amarillo. Gay guys would hold the door open for you and not expect you to split the bill. Occasionally you might meet an actual straight man with them when their little brother or college roommate was visiting. Or the straight black stud who was gay-friendly might end the evening with one of their girls. If you put on a few pounds or wore a dress twice, gay men would scarcely notice. All they required is that you should be "fun." Lonely, beautiful women who were staying true to a fiancé in another city were attractive eye candy. In the old days before AIDS and before gays were so identifiable, a beautiful gal pal might lure a drunk heterosexual man into a three-way, especially desirable in the distant past when gays were attracted only to straights ("Why would I go to bed with another pansy? And do what? Rub pussies?").

In those bad old days (the fifties), gay men were allergic to women, but in the seventies, after Stonewall, gay men started hanging out with women, just as after the feminist-revolution women began to socialize with one another. I can remember in the 1940s when my mother thought it was an admission of defeat (or perversion) to be seen in public alone with another woman. Now gay men search out their female counterparts; an Australian friend is hosting a woman from Berlin who, he says, "is a real slut—just like me!" My husband has a rich young lady friend who is a lesbian but currently with a man. My late best friend Marilyn used to say she preferred sex with men but that she could fall in love only with a woman.

Jim

I ALWAYS SAY THAT THE GREAT LOVE of my life was Jim Ruddy. One day a tall blond, slender and with a booming bass voice, rang my bell. He'd tricked with Stan and at first thought I was Stan, though in no way were Stan and I alike and that should have been my first clue that he was slightly crazy. He was a student at NYU. He was eerily friendly, a handsome wide-eyed Midwesterner, someone who smelled good when he embraced me and pulled out his large penis, which slanted off to one side.

We were twenty-three.

He was a swimmer and a good, long-distance one, with the long muscles, slender waist, round buttocks, and powerful legs to prove it. He nodded at everything I said. He had a smiling, courteous manner, as if he'd just stepped out of a time machine from the eighteenth century and from a distant, politer country. He wanted to be liked and nothing could be easier. He had no filter. Irony was wasted on him because he believed everything he heard. He wanted a mentor. I wanted a husband. No matter what one said, he said, "Is that right?"

Once after seeing an emotional French movie, *Sundays and Cybèle*, the kind only a young person can love, Jim and I were so excited we ran and ran through the nearly empty midnight streets. We crossed over to the East River by an overpass on the Upper East Side and kept running. I was so full of nameless emotion; that must have been the happiest moment of my life. An ecstasy of just feeling young and alive that I shared with Jim. Of course at the time someone doesn't think, I'm young and alive. I thought I would be this happy and energetic forever, that only morally compromised people got old. We said we wanted to live hard, die young, and leave a beautiful body. In the 1960s we said you should never trust anyone over thirty. My lungs were scorched from all the air I'd swallowed. The water was sliding by in the darkness, faceted and black as coal.

I was going to an enormous sibyl of a shrink who sat in a Barcalounger on which she presented her fat legs. She smoked seriously and surveyed her homosexual with her agate eyes under heavy lids. She seldom spoke. If I burst into tears, she sat upright and pushed Kleenex toward me then reclined again.

I was too openly gay for Jim. Not *camp* (the English writer Adam Mars-Jones said I was the least camp person he'd ever known). But gay, even in those years before Stonewall. Like everyone except drag queens, I suppose, I said I wanted to go straight. I was determined to be a great writer—not bestselling but canonical—and I thought, this being before tell-all biographies were written, that all great writers were straight. Tolstoy was the best example. No matter that he was rabidly unfaithful, that he pressured his wife and children to be severe anti-materialists, to labor beside the peasants and not enjoy the privileges of their caste. No matter that he forced his ideals on them, that they had to be pacifists, scorn the imperial court, be humble and Christian, his daughters had to forgo a debut, his son couldn't become an officer, his wife had to guide the plow and feed hordes of seedy Tolstoyans. He, like all the greats, had a wife and children and could write with uncanny detail about them. I was just an immature homosexual caught in the oral aggressive stage, unable to flower as a full genital. We had no feminist or race-based analysis; we were sentimental socialists, opposed to the great powers no matter where they lurked, reverential before Ho Chi Minh, still ready to dismiss the bad news coming out of the Soviet Union as the invention of the unreliable capitalist press. Like all Americans we were obsessed with our American lifestyles and identity politics—even then, in the sixties, though those preoccupations were all mixed up with our crude leftism and doctrinaire Freudianism, ideas that couldn't be squared but were in the air and I, at least, wasn't a systematic thinker. Or much of a thinker at all.

Jim was a thinker, not critical but curious. He never analyzed anything nor was he skeptical. He just engulfed every subject and had a keen memory. He liked to talk about the content of books, not what students today call "theory."

I encouraged Jim to deal with his problems in therapy—with my shrink! Soon he was mad as a hatter (hatters, if you didn't know, actually went mad from the chemicals used to work felt). He had "bizarre somatic delusions"—that is, he thought his arms were on fire. His energy was torrential and he'd run up and down six flights of stairs back and forth until you distracted him. He laughed his booming laugh as if only he had caught the joke but it was a real corker. The laugh, as in a Francis Bacon painting, would turn into a demonic howl. His emotions were very "labile."

Jim had fallen for a handsome man, Sam McDonnell, in his thirties who owned a whole building near the foot of Christopher Street, which he was slowly restoring for his bride-to-be. Jim loved him for his unsmiling gravity, his muscular hairy body, his red hair, and his dawning heterosexuality. I think they cuddled like brothers, but Jim was too crazy to sleep. All night he paced the building site with its reinforced beams, its shaky metal scaffolding, its giant uninstalled sheets of glass, its buckets of tar and oil paint, its temporary stairs, its inch of water in the basement. Frances, our shrink, committed Jim to the psych ward at a nearby hospital. I would try to talk sense to Jim with no success, then Sam would take over. Sam and I met and exchanged phone numbers and would talk deep into the night—one o'clock, two o'clock, three—about Jim. Sam thought Jim just needed to pull himself together. I was given to pathologizing him. I called an old friend who'd been committed to some of the most expensive mental hospitals and asked how to get Jim out of there. He said, "Jim has to befriend the other patients and pretend to be sane. Talk to them. Show interest. Crazy people are isolated. Try to organize round-the-clock group therapy with anyone willing to try." I passed this advice along, but the sibylline shrink Frances had stopped visiting him and handed him over to a staff therapist at the hospital, a young brunette who wore fatiguing amounts of rose essence. You could smell her two wards away. She sent him to a famous hospital in Minneapolis, where he stayed for a year.

Sam and I continued to talk together over the phone. Sometimes I'd be in bed sleeping when he called. I liked his voice. Sometimes I'd fall back to sleep while his rich baritone kept flowing over the cradled receiver. But since neither of us had news of Jim, our calls became less and less frequent and less obsessive. I suppose Sam finished restoring his house and married his fiancée. I never heard from him again.

Jim was cured and got a doctorate from Rutgers. He had sex with me one more time before he became a faithful lover of Miguel Algarín, the founder of the Nuyorican Poets Café. I was asked by the *New York Times* to review an "important" book by José Lezama Lima, a Cuban whose *Paradiso* told of a day in the life of a gay man in Havana written in parodies of every European literary genre since the Middle Ages. Jim was getting a PhD in comparative literature and I asked him to help me track down the various original texts Lezama Lima was imitating, reviewing the book was as if one were handed Joyce's *Ulysses* on publication and asked to turn in two thousand words on it in three weeks. Jim helped me a lot and as a result I sounded much more cultured than I was. The dismissive review in the *New York Review of Books* said that *Paradiso* read like *À la recherche* written not by Proust but by pedantic Bloch, though most people throughout the cultured world consider it a neo-baroque masterpiece and the first work of magical realism in South America. Although Lezama Lima was invited to give lectures throughout Europe and South America, the Cuban regime would not grant him an exit visa.

I gave Jim the idea for his dissertation. He treated me with great formality and tenderness; he had no money but

I remember how he came in from New Jersey and took me out to an excellent French restaurant. I wanted more sex and less ceremony, but I was content *faute de mieux* to be treated so deferentially.

Miguel had a whole cult around him. Jim and Miguel must have split; Jim eventually ended up with a big bearded man and they went off to California to the mountains to open a ski resort. I wrote a novel about Jim, *The Beautiful Room Is Empty.* While I was teaching at Brown in 1990, I got a letter from his lover who said that Jim had died of AIDS. He said Jim had read my novel and been pleased by it. And that was that.

When I speak of the great love of my life, I don't mean the degree to which someone loved *me.* I mean how madly, desperately *I* was in love. Once when I was sobbing in public over my broken heart over some man or another, Joyce Carol Oates, friend and colleague at Princeton, asked me coolly how many men had I rejected and hurt? Of course in my egotism I hadn't kept track of that, though they must have been in the dozens. For me love was always passionate and one-sided, aspirational and impossible, never domestic and mutual. Did I need that distance, that anguish, to contemplate the beloved and write about him? When Jim went crazy and ran up and down the psych ward convinced his arms were on fire, I kept wondering what I must have said. It was always about me, some lack or evil or mistake in me, my failure to be lovable. Now in the cold polar heart of old age I look at all my travails in love as comical and pointless, repetitious and dishonorable.

* * *

I USED TO BE SHOCKED when Virgil Thomson the composer—who wrote the opera *Four Saints in Three Acts* with Gertrude Stein, which received its premiere in 1934 with an all-black cast—used to be called to the telephone. I knew him in the 1970s when he was almost in his eighties; he'd come back to the table and say, "Well, Smitty is dead," and just sit down and continue the conversation about something else. I was amazed that he could receive the news with such indifference about such a close friend.

Now that I'm in my eighties I realize his emotion was stoicism, not indifference; someone who outlives his contemporaries knows that he very likely will be next but that for the moment "he controls the narrative," as pundits say. When you get to be old, everyone consults you about the biographies of your famous contemporaries. You get the last word, at least until the dead person's *Complete Letters* come out.

A life, a love. I always say that Jim Ruddy was the great love of my life. What does that mean now he's just a faint neural scratch on my brain? It seems the hippocampus delegates short-term memories to various other neurons, where they are encoded forever. Does that mean an electrode stimulating the right neurons could make Jim, his conversation, his deep voice, his big curved penis, as real as it was fifty or sixty years ago, a hologram? The wondering way he'd greet any declaration with a tentative acceptance? His always saying "Is that right?" no matter how preposterous one's remark had been.

Maybe I've forgotten him because I wrote about him; I've always thought that writing about someone is the kiss-off. Nabokov, in *Speak, Memory*, was apprehensive about writing about his nanny since he liked revisiting her in his thoughts and he knew once he'd committed her to print, he'd lose her. Some people wonder why I've not written about them. If they're a current part of my life, I need to keep them on life support; my husband is Michael Carroll, whom I've been with since 1995. I've never written about him; he's too precious to me. My recent fiction is less autobiography and more thought experiment. I assemble my monsters from stolen body parts (his nape, her stutter). Often I want to lead the reader to a better (more compassionate, more forgiving, bolder, more loving) world by picturing it as if it already existed; George Meredith called that process "moral sculpture."

What did it feel like to be in love?

Constant suspense. Does he love me yet? More? Less? Is he getting bored?

I always fell in love with the wrong person. Proust advises that falling in love means falling in love with the wrong person.

In college I used to slow dance with athletes at a party in someone's living room; I liked to feel their hard-ons pressing into me, to feel their muscles under their cashmere sweaters, to smell the mixture of cigarettes and English Leather cologne. Maybe because I was already twenty-nine when Stonewall took place, I was never gay and proud. I coauthored *The Joy of Gay Sex* and encouraged everyone else to be self-accepting, but I never was.

Later I discovered that people had thought of me as "hot," but at the time, when I actually was hot, I hated myself. My cock was too small, a trick told me my mouth stank of rot, there was always an inch of flab around my waist. I had my hair straightened for the surfer look, in France I had fat suctioned off my stomach by a surgeon, then I wore a leather corset for a month. I was always fighting my weight—doctors, speed, fasting for twenty days in a Swiss clinic. Cabbage soup for a week. Lunch and dinner. No carbs. The Atkins diet. The Scarsdale diet. The grapefruit diet. The gym-four-nights-a-week diet. The white-wine-and-steak diet.

I could never see the problems beautiful men had. To me they were gods who had nothing to complain of. I couldn't see they were frustrated in their careers. Or that they were hooked on drugs. Or that they felt intimidated by me, of all people. Or that they were lonely or afraid. In the 1960s a drag queen named Brandy Alexander said to me, "Oh, Ed White, you're the universal ball." A female literary agent told me, "We all wanted you back then." I found out years later a killingly handsome and accomplished friend of mine had tried to make me his partner. When I, groggy and self-hating as usual, hadn't picked up on his overtures, he'd ended up with someone else, a friend of mine, almost a double.

Did I always endure unreciprocated love because I could only love (and write about it) when I was rejected? Did my low self-esteem seek out rejection, as in I wouldn't want to belong to any club that would accept me? Or does everyone hope to trade up to a newer, better lover? Not social climbers but amorous climbers?

Maybe my values were skewed by elite gay resorts such as Fire Island, where everyone was a handsome bodybuilder and corporate lawyer or celebrated doctor, where men were as sexy as gigolos in Saint-Tropez but not for hire. In that world every guy had to be as beautiful as a woman and as successful as a man—that is, a Manhattan woman or man. Fire Island was a race no one was winning. Everyone next summer was a year older, hair grayer, their crow's-feet engraved deeper into eagle claws. Sure, the Velvet Mafia would always have nineteen-year-olds naked in their Olympic-size pool or dining at midnight at their long refectory table, food prepared by a private chef. They would always have their panty-melting drugs, would be supervising wrestling matches of their Cuban bodybuilders in the surf, their guests worrying about their depilated torsos, laughing with their unblemished teeth, the braided-cord tattoo around a huge wet biceps, thick as a magnum of champagne, all traits they'd only recently acquired.

I've always been bewitched by physical beauty, masculinity, and erudition. Jim was the perfect embodiment of those qualities. I may be the last person alive who loved him. His earlier lovers are all dead. I have a heartbreaking photo of him on the beach at Riis Park. Looking pouty and exquisite with his long legs, flat stomach, and full head of copper hair, scrutinizing the world as if it were surprising, maybe hostile.

Rilke has a beautiful poem about looking at a daguerreotype of his long-dead father as a cadet (here translated by my oldest friend, Alfred Corn):

Portrait of My Father in Early Youth

In his eye: dream. The forehead as though in
touch
with something distant. As for the mouth,
immense
youth, unsmiling seductiveness,
and before the slim and noble uniform's
highly ornamental braid,
the saber's meshwork hilt, with both hands
waiting, at rest, constrained to do nothing,
and now no longer quite visible, as though,
earliest to reach for what's distant, they're
vanishing.
And all the rest so enswathed within itself,

so erased, it's as if, deeply shadowed
by its own depth, we can't understand it.
You, fast-disappearing daguerreotype,
in my more slowly disappearing hands.

Harold

I'VE OFTEN THOUGHT I SHOULD look up my old neighbor Harold, whom my nephew interviewed when Harold was in his sixties. He was still in Cincinnati, running the family business, married with children and grandchildren. My nephew came away from the interview (he was thinking of writing my biography) with only one astounding statement: Harold said my father, Mr. White, was the kindest man he'd ever known. I'd always presented my father in my writing as a maniac, a misanthrope, a cruel bastard, a bore. Apparently Mr. White taught Harold how to play baseball, took him to Cincinnati the Reds games and also to symphonies. By contrast, my father had always been in a rage with me; perhaps he was appalled I was such a sissy, interested in books but not in baseball (the world's most boring game, though I admit baseball players are sexy with their big butts, dirty white uniforms, and chewing tobacco). To toughen me up my father always had me mowing the lawn in the Cincinnati summer equatorial heat or stacking boxes of copper tubing in his airless warehouse, which smelled of melting tar.

Harold was enough of a sissy for my stepmother and me to get him into a green slip and makeup for Halloween. I lived with my father in seventh grade, as the divorce agreement specified. My mother, who was a psychologist, thought I needed a male model. I agreed, but my under-exercised father scarcely struck me as the sort of model I had in mind. My father's house was a four-bedroom Spanish-style villa of the 1920s built around a courtyard in which there was a fountain, the water pouring out of the mouth of a dolphin held in the arms of a naked male child. It was so hot and muggy that few flowers could grow other than dahlias, marigolds, zinnias, and geraniums, redolent of the dry dirt.

Harold wore braces and was tall and weedy, smelled of acne medication, and embodied the "Yes, sir," "No, ma'am" variety of 1950s politeness. We were all polite back then—that's how you could tell who was middle-class. Maybe we kids could manage to be polite to our elders since we so seldom saw them. Bleating and blushing, we pushed past them in the hallway and hung out with other teens. It was during that era that adolescence was invented. In French movies of the period such as the

Cocteau-Melville *Les Enfants terribles*, youngsters moved out of the nursery in short pants directly into sex intrigues and tuxedos. But in American movies such as *Rebel Without a Cause*, teens squeezed in jeans raced around in cars, unsupervised, their hair thick with product, their kisses luminescent in Technicolor. There was even a hint of the homo sidekick, Plato, who of course had to die. Later, we had causes—against the war, for Mao—but at first we were just teen rebels, neither child nor adult, our predominant feature being that we were somehow misunderstood.

Harold was no sort of rebel. He was shy and sweet, he had an indoor complexion, an overbite, and a weak chin. He was pleasant to everyone—not more so to one, not less to others. He'd grown very tall, taller than my father, but he hunched his shoulders as if being tall were an impertinence. He did his chores around his house without grumbling. I never met—or even saw—his parents.

My room was at the end of a carpeted hall and over the garage. How many times I would psychoanalyze the moonlit branches outside my window and imagine an adult lover whose lust-o-meter could detect even at a distance that behind that precise window was a thirteen-year-old boy with a hard dick and a yearning to be abducted. In one of James Merrill's poems, he hears as a child about rich kids being kidnapped and he hopes he'll be taken away by "Floyd." I had the same desire and wrote a sonnet that began, "Because I loved you before I met you . . ." Although I was worried about the inconvenient trochees, the verse expressed a real sentiment I had. I'd discovered masturbation (which will always be associated with the smell of a mildewed washcloth in my mind, since I must have first jerked off in my bathroom, the only room with a door that locked) and my fantasies were all about a lord, an English lord, not a backcountry Floyd with a cigarette behind his ear, a lord whose heart would guide him up the branches and into my waiting arms and then spirit me away in the waiting Rolls. My fantasies were all prologue, as if even then I suspected the third act would inevitably be a disappointment and need not be imagined.

Meanwhile all I had at hand was Harold—shy, smiling Harold with his food-gummed braces and cold hands. I began to wrestle him one day and noticed he was aroused. I tried to pull his trousers down off his skinny hips and he started giggling as if I were tickling him: "Stop! Stop!" he murmured between giggles as he twisted from side to side.

I didn't really like him and felt free to manhandle him, though he was taller and stronger than I. Now I know I should have been afraid I was exploiting him, using him, failing to respect his limits. He was hard, but of course someone can be excited and repulsed.

I'd cornholed a boy or two and knew it could be done.

I had his trousers off by now and he was fully erect, enough bodily yea-saying for me.

"You know guys stick it in each other's holes?"

"Ow. Doesn't that hurt?"

"Not if you go slow and use Vaseline."

"But what if it's all icky in there?"

"It isn't usually. We could take turns. You could cornhole me first."

"Cornhole?"

"That's what you call it when you stick it in a fella's rear end."

"Why?"

I ignored him. My idea was that I'd cum first. Since I was the queerer of us, I could stay interested even after my climax, whereas I doubted he could.

Harold lay on his stomach, his head to one side and pillowed on his bent arm. I tried to find something sexy about his nape or his ears (the things that usually turn me on), but his nape was shaggy and his lobes were seamlessly attached to his jawline. His buttocks were loose and jiggly and cold, like balloons half filled with ice water.

I found his asshole and loosened it with Vaseline on my finger.

"That feels weird. It feels like I have to go potty."

"It always feels like that at first," I said confidently. I pushed the head of my penis into his crack.

"Ouch. That hurts." I could see—and smell—the tuna fish clinging to his braces.

"Just relax. Don't be such a baby."

"No, it really hurts! Take it out!"

I pulled out and sighed impatiently. We lay there in silence, his eyelash brushing against the pillow like a captive firefly. A full minute went by. I was sure my pillowcase would smell of tuna fish later.

"I promise you," I said, "it won't hurt this time."

Harold was noncommittal. I couldn't read from the half of his face that was visible either assent or dissent. As gently as possible, I pushed and it went right in.

It felt better than anything, a warm, wet, tight glove. I didn't exactly plunge (it would be years before I'd be taught to do that) but just "muddled," as bartenders say when they crush a sugar cube on mint leaves and bitters.

"Hurry up," Harold said.

"Hold your horses. I'm almost ready!"

"Did you squirt inside me?" he asked indignantly.

"What's the big deal? You're not going to get pregnant."

"I don't want that stuff inside me." He went down the hall to sit on the toilet.

"Don't take all day," I called out.

He shushed me.

And then he came back to claim his pound of flesh. I was a much braver soldier than he'd been. It never occurred to me that any guy could enjoy being cornholed; the pleasure, obviously, was all in the fucking.

Although Harold was the Catholic, he seemed much less guilt ridden than I and soon he was coming by every afternoon as I practiced the piano. He would stand behind me. He'd stand closer and closer until he'd be rubbing his erection against my shoulder blade, my undernourished wing. When I'd stop playing, though my hands were still on the keys, I'd look up at him and he'd be smiling in a sweet, fuzzy way and gently entreating, "Come on, let's go upstairs to your room, please."

I didn't know what I was feeling beyond irritation, but the snake in the basket wanted to stand upright on his tail, though I had to reach down to pull him free of my underpants. Harold covered my hand with his and said passionately, "Only for a minute."

Upstairs we undressed in silence. Within seconds I had vaselined my finger and inserted it. Inside I could feel a big, hard BM, which oddly enough didn't make me squeamish. If anything, it excited me if I could figure a way to navigate around it and if he didn't start complaining it hurt. When I was in fifth grade a classmate with blond hair, a juicy smile, and a Southern accent had sat on my lap on a park bench and rubbed his butt around on my dick and said, in a phony high voice, "Oh, darling," and laughed. It was a parody of a movie, I guess. Then he'd led me into a nearby two-car garage that sat out behind an old wooden house. There he'd lost interest in fooling around with me, but he'd lowered his trousers, squatted, and taken a big shit. The rich, steamy odor filled the closed garage, turning it into a stable. He found an oil-stained newspaper to wipe with. He was grinning like crazy as if he'd gotten away with something big. Ever after, the smell of shit fascinated me, not to the point of a fetish I sought out or paid extra for, but as a sort of booster shot for an inoculation that was already efficacious. Like all revolting things, it was horrid until it wasn't.

Almost every afternoon I fucked Harold and then he fucked me. Every time I promised myself I wouldn't do it again. I thought even jerking off was a fault and I always vowed that this time, this time would be the last. But then Harold was rubbing up against me and looking at me misty-eyed with lust (which in his family—who knows?—might have been confused with tenderness). We Whites liked our lust straight, right out of the tube.

I know I'm contradicting myself. In the foreword I said I'd always felt some tenderness toward a sex partner, but in this case I felt contempt for Harold's cowardice, his squeamishness, paired as it was with unrelenting daily lust.

And then one afternoon the maid walked in on us just as I was pulling out of Harold and reaching for a wet washcloth. We were naked except for our socks.

Later that day, after dinner, my father went off to his den to smoke his pipe. As I started to rush off to my bathroom to jerk off again, my stepmother said, "Eddie, Lila told me—"

"I know, I know," I said irritably. "We'll never try that again."

"Well, see that you don't. It surprises me that a nice boy like Harold would go in for that sort of nastiness." I noticed my viciousness didn't surprise her at all.

Years later, when we were eighteen, Harold got me alone upstairs in his room during a party and fished out of his fly an enormous penis, like a thick roll of lard. He wanted to fuck me with it. He was smiling a braceless smile and pulled longingly at my clothes. Indignant, I said, "You want to put that monster in me? No way. How did it get so big?"

I've always regretted my refusal.

I had a gay shrink who said gay boys are always complaining their fathers rejected them. But often as not, the boys reject their straight fathers, who don't provide the kind of tenderness the boys crave.

That made sense to me. My father—who was neurotically competitive in sports, determined to win even when playing basketball with his nine-year-old grandson—would have loved the rough-and-tumble of a good game with me. Harold satisfied that urge in him much more than I could, his poetry-writing, piano-playing sissy son. My athletic sister could cater to his athleticism, which in any event was more aspirational than an active force in his life. He was the kind of man who followed sports just enough to complain about the Red Sox at the barbershop or hazard an opinion about that trade between the Yankees and the Orioles. He really wasn't a man's man or anybody's man. He liked sleeping all day and working all night while Brahms's violin concerto played on the big blond mahogany record player. He could spend hours and hours whittling his nails with the dozen gleaming instruments in their rectangular ostrich-skin case that zipped closed on three sides. He might take a break at dawn to walk his dog through the sleeping, lightless neighborhood. At this peaceful hour, after a satisfying lonely night at the calculator, he might switch from his illegally imported Cuban cigars to a mellow Brahmsian pipe. He was the loneliest man in the world and didn't seem to notice it. I'm more like my mother—crying over men, fighting my weight, deploying my misguided Southern charm—but in my inherited character, I can detect my father's little icy heart.

Becky

When I was in my twenties, I worked on the thirty-second floor of a midtown office building that must have looked bleak to visitors but of course for us was warm and human with intrigues and flirtations, with rigid precedence uncomfortably disguised by American egalitarianism (our grizzled boss we had to call Hal, a Korean War pilot), and by watercooler dramas. It was 1965 and I was twenty-five and in therapy to go straight.

There was a tall, blond, nearly comatose copyboy who "showed basket," as we gays would say of a big visible crotch. He pushed his cart all over the thirty-second floor with its prestigious offices with windows and its humiliating little sunless interior cubicles and delivered mail and flyers and drafts of the columns we wrote for our publications. He once confessed to me in a nearly flatline voice that almost every man and woman on our floor had propositioned him. Once his live-in lover discovered him in bed with someone else and knocked him about until he lost the sight of one eye. "It's okay," he said, accentuating the positive, "I've still got another one."

I fooled around with him on the landing behind a fire door; we couldn't get back in and had to bang on the door until someone with a knowing smile saved us.

As mentioned, everyone back then wanted me apparently. I had no idea; women's interest in me was especially invisible (though one beautiful woman had asked me home one autumn afternoon in Riverside Park). There was a warm, impulsive girl on my floor with lovely hairless legs who would lean seriously into the conversation, then suddenly grin, self-consciously, as if she'd just remembered not to presume, that she was only a girl. Her name was Becky and she was almost always barefoot inside, even in winter. Her legs, often folded under a full skirt, seemed starved for a tan.

She would sit on the carpet next to my rolling office chair and lean her head from left to right like a not thoroughly exact metronome. She would laugh, ask oddball questions, smile as a slow, cloudy aftereffect of something I'd said, then unaccountably get up and leave, almost as if to prove her independence, or in a hippie obedience to her psychological circadian rhythms. Or had I somehow offended her or bored her?

In March she invited me for the weekend to her parents' beach house in the Hamptons. I worried about my clothes. I had a blazer I'd bought on time (twelve payments of ten dollars a month). I had chinos and penny loafers. I had a blue V-neck wool sweater that smelled of damp. My briefs were theoretically white but actually a bit gray; one pair had a broken elastic that dangled down my thigh. My socks were green wool with no holes but balding patches. Should I bring a bottle of Scotch as a house gift? What if they didn't drink? Once I'd given some expensive perfume to be heated in a terra-cotta ring on a light bulb to an architect who, it turned out, didn't have a single old-fashioned bulb in his ultramodern house.

Her parents were nice. Her mother had been a modern dancer and still moved fluidly and was usually barefoot as well, her feet large and blue-white with a visibly high instep. She'd studied with Martha Graham. The father was a broker with a white bottlebrush mustache and a citrusy cologne that became stronger in the closed car. He had lovely manners but the patience in his voice sounded strained, provisional, as if *his* father had taught him to edit out his innate irritation.

Their white clapboard house with the green shutters stood on, I guessed, one and a half acres planted with old trees and flowering hydrangea bushes, which I preferred to call to myself by their French name, *hortensie*, which seemed to go better with their matronly look. Inside were three big couches covered with wine-stained chintz printed with big pink peonies. The dog stretched out on one couch with his head resting on the upholstered arm rubbed thin. He was a medium-size collie with a noble face that longed for a pince-nez.

Becky was good about showing me my big white room with a double bed draped in white chenille, a Platonic chair, and a glassed-in dark-wood bookcase filled with sun-bleached books. She gave me my towel and washcloth with an ironic curtsy.

At the table that evening—while the late sun illuminated the big garden in pink and blue lights just outside the windows, as if it were a set for a summer play by Turgenev—the father carved the big roast chicken and the mother served mashed potatoes and asparagus, a curiously hearty meal given the season and the slenderness of my hosts. We each had a napkin in napkin rings painted like Russian Easter eggs in shiny swirls. "This house has such a wonderful spirit—has it been in the family a long time?" I asked Becky's parents impartially, as if they were not married but siblings, which seemed less controversial.

There followed some details about a childless great-aunt and a botched marriage in the 1950s, but I was too conscious of my impersonation of a gentleman and my shabby clothes to pay much attention. I was especially humbled by my sudden reverting to an uncorrected Midwestern mispronunciation of *wash* as *warsh* and my failure to say *anywhere* as *ennuh-ware*, though I'd learned the correct mandarin way of saying that shibboleth only last week from my *Mayflower* office mate.

That night I had every intention of sneaking into Becky's room when everyone was asleep (her parents' room was on a different floor), but I became totally absorbed in a book some earlier guest had left behind, stories about corrupt priests, which I kept reading though I was in my better pair of underpants on top of the chenille bedspread and hard from time to time. After I'd finished another story, it was one thirty—too late. I turned off my light and jacked off, thinking of various male body parts.

I was heading off to Málaga even though Franco was still in power and we weren't supposed to visit Spain. Becky and I decided to meet up in Paris. She would come to my hotel on the Île Saint-Louis at a certain hour on a given day (in those pre-cell-phone days even flaky people had to make precise plans).

I'd chosen Málaga for my first trip to Europe because it was supposed to be sunny and inexpensive. When I stepped out of the plane, I was floored by the heat and realized I'd brought the wrong clothes. It seemed my early twenties were all about the wrong clothes. My hotel, small and whitewashed, was called La Gaviota, which the clerk told me meant "birdcage" but actually meant "seagull," when I looked it up. The hotel had given my room away. I stood there sweating in my wool suit while the English-challenged, shellac-haired clerk found me a room with a shared bath in his aunt's house. The house was nearby. The whole area seemed under construction and I walked in my cheap black shoes (I'd heard a gentleman, alas, is always judged by his shoes) through freshly plowed orange mud and the concrete foundations of unfinished buildings sprouting metal rods rusting over the concrete. I walked past big bushes of flowering purple bougainvillea as I held my cheap Fourteenth Street luggage, purple polyester; I was nearly felled by sleep deprivation.

Although Becky and I had gone in for heavy petting on the unlit porch that Saturday night and I'd actually gotten two fingers into that molten honeypot and her hand had brushed my erect penis, we hadn't gone "all the way." But we'd agreed we'd consummate things in Paris, which sounded scary and romantic. Not too scary because I'd actually had an erection on the porch. I kept thinking I was rounding a corner sexually and that filled me with cautious glee. I'd be normal and could marry, father children, get a promotion (married guys rose quicker at the office). I'd have someone to accompany me into old age. As a genuine heterosexual I could write novels with a universal appeal. I just had to stay out of trouble here in Spain, although I'd already heard about a nude gay beach in Torremolinos (a town "of no cultural interest," according to my guidebook). A guy I'd picked up in New York had talked about the "action" in a cave there ("But don't get trapped by the high tide"). I'd found out a bus went there.

I debated with myself whether to make the trip. I couldn't reform overnight, could I?

I did go, and when we got into Torremolinos, I said to the bus driver the word I'd looked up, *playa*, meaning "beach." He didn't indicate with his dark glasses and belly pressed into the big steering wheel that he'd heard me, but he left me off at the right place, the gay beach, I noticed, not looking at me as I stepped down in a great reproach of hissing brakes.

I fooled around in the cave with a balding man who came in my hand, which I washed away in the seawater. I was still fully clothed in my black wool trousers. I waited for an hour for the return bus. It was driven by the same man, who punched my ticket without looking at me.

That night in bed (a room had finally opened up at La Gaviota) I guided my masturbation thoughts penitently toward Becky and away from the man in the cave, whose penis had been stubby with a purple glans where the prepuce had been pulled back. His pubes were mostly white. I kissed my pillow, on which I conjured up her sweet lips, as soft as frequently washed linen.

I had no friends there. What had I been thinking when I chose Málaga for my maiden voyage to Europe? The only people I spoke to were the desk clerk whose aunt I'd stayed with and the Gypsy waiter, who spoke French to the family of four and English to me. He wore a red jacket with gold epaulets, a clip-on black bow tie, and a white dress shirt that I suspected had been "ironed" by being folded carefully every night under his mattress. His hair and sideburns were dyed as black as rubber tires.

Once I'd eaten my dinner, I had nothing to do. I'd read all the stories in the priest book, which I'd stolen, and leafed through the old French and German magazines in the lobby (at that point I knew no foreign languages except Chinese). I went walking down the orange-mud road into town. A Gypsy boy threw his shoeshine box down in my path and began to hammer metal taps into the heels of my shoes. I told him to stop but didn't have the vocabulary. In a second he'd finished the assault, helped me slide back into my loafers, and held out a little dirty hand to be paid. I gave him a few pesetas but he whined so loudly in automatic protest that I produced a few more. He kept running after me as I clacked along in my violated shoes; he shoved his hand at me until he gave up and walked away expressionlessly on the lookout for a new victim.

The little botanical park had winding paths under a heavy, hot canopy of tropical leaves. It smelled of rusty water, though the bench where I settled was dry. Two teens, tall and blond, walked past and looked at me curiously. I thought they were foreigners until I heard them speaking Spanish in their unnaturally bass voices; everyone male in Málaga had practiced having a low voice. Soon after, like a porpoise following minnows, a chubby Spaniard came down the path and sat next to me, smiled, and held out a warm hand, a worker's hand, to be shaken. He held my hand a second too long and his middle finger stroked my palm. He reeked of toilet water and scooched down and spread his legs until I could see his growing erection. I stared at his crotch until he took my hand and pushed it onto the thickening brawn ticking up to its full length. We smiled and he jerked with his head in the direction farther down the path. We both stood tentatively, he put a hand on my butt and pushed me the right way. He mumbled something I didn't understand. I nodded with a smile.

Soon we reached the bullring and he positioned me with my back to the giant structure, which smelled of manure. It was very dark. Tattered posters announcing past and future bullfights covered the high gray windowless walls; there were chain-locked wooden doors, battered and flaking paint. No one was around. The man began to kiss me. I felt for his cock and it was soft. His heart was pounding. His hand was on my back and then I realized he had a knife poking between my shoulder blades. Oh, that's why now he couldn't get hard and his mouth was dry.

He slid my wallet out of my back right pocket, stepped away, darting an eye at me every few seconds. He took all the bills from the wallet and threw the rifled square of synthetic snakeskin at my feet. Luckily he hadn't taken my credit cards or passport or driver's license. He walked briskly away. I retrieved my wallet, went in the same direction, discovered him sitting on a bench on one side of a dusty circle of grass. I sat on a bench on the opposite side and looked at him. The light above us buzzed alive, died, turned on, buzzed, went off.

He and I both knew that in Franco's Spain homosexuality was a more serious crime than theft. I was powerless. Why did I keep sitting there and staring at him as he briefly materialized and disappeared in the buzzing light? I thought, he can't kill me and I can't denounce him. We were deadlocked.

Minutes went by. It was hot. I was sweating. The two Spanish teens cruised by again.

The man waved me over and I slowly crossed the dusty circle and sat beside him. He offered me half a stick of chewing gum. After another long moment he pointed to me, then to himself, and slid his right forefinger obscenely into a circle he'd made of his left thumb and middle finger. I shrugged and smiled. "Porque no?"

I followed him into a shallow cave let into the side of a hillock. This was a botanical garden after all; each of the trees had a little metal name tag stuck in the ground identifying it. The man pulled my wool trousers down, spit into his palm, lubricated his penis, and stuck it in. Five strokes and he was done, had buttoned up and disappeared into the night. I thought, at least I got my money's worth, though I hadn't. I changed new traveler's checks the next morning at La Gaviota.

I worried that now I was soiled for Paris and Becky. What if he'd given me crabs? The clap? I wondered, could clap in the ass be transmitted through the penis? Was it a generalized disease or localized? In New York I'd had clap in the ass twice and crabs many times. I looked for the telltale signs, a haze of mucus clinging to the stool and frequent farting for anal gonorrhea; itching lice at the base of pubic hair, especially along the blood-rich root of the penis. If you scraped your fingernail where it itched, sometimes you could dislodge a crab and watch it wriggle semi transparently at the end of your fingernail. I'd heard that in Spain you could buy penicillin pills without a prescription at the pharmacy, but I was afraid a weak dose would just mask the condition.

★ ★ ★

I FLEW TO PARIS AND took a taxi in and found my hotel as charming as Becky had promised. She was due to arrive the next day; we were getting together at three in the afternoon. She had a room on the same floor. I walked around the Île Saint-Louis, crossed over to the Île de la Cité, and entered Notre Dame. I bobbed a curtsy and sketched in the sign of the cross, though I didn't really know how to do it (I'd been brought up Protestant).

I'd heard there was a small, trendy gay bar called Le Fiacre in Saint-Germain. I thought I should see it, though just as research; I was saving what was left of me for Becky. The entrance was on a side street and utterly anonymous. When I rang the bell, an older man in a tuxedo opened; he was wearing a large white plastic earring and announced he was an *eepee*. I finally figured out he was pretending to be a hippie and he imagined they wore earrings. A French song came on the jukebox, "Hippie Hippie Hourrah." I thought about how we should love everything now that we were hippies. The proprietor with his earring demonstrated this new philosophy by kissing cute customers on the cheek and rearing back in gales of laughter, his hands held up like claws. No one looked at me. I went upstairs, where I was just as invisible. The hippie song came back on for the third time. I slipped out after one *scotch et soda*, ten dollars. I walked home in my shoes still outfitted with their taps, tapping along the deserted foggy streets. I tried to judge by my farts how infected I was. My poop in the morning didn't seem to be veiled with mucus and it didn't hurt to shit.

Finally Becky arrived and seemed disappointed to see me. I was equally indifferent to her. She looked very French to me—a skillfully draped scarf, black blouse and skirt, no jewelry, pale white lipstick and winged eyes, her shoulder-length hair cut in Juliette Gréco bangs. I saw that she was embarrassed by me, my wool trousers, cheap clacking shoes, baggy shirt, horn-rim glasses. I couldn't speak French. I told her how everyone wanted to be a hippie but had odd notions of what that consisted of. She said, "Groovy," sarcastically. I said I dug her threads. She asked me if in Spain I'd visited the Alhambra or Seville. I hadn't. I had done nothing interesting in Spain. She seemed shocked that I was so incurious culturally. That evening we sat silently in a sidewalk café in Saint-Germain. I gathered she didn't want to be overheard speaking English. Eventually I got up, paid for our drinks, and clacked back to the Île Saint-Louis. Becky said she'd see me in the morning. Maybe we'd go to the Louvre. We never did.

I guessed I was gay after all.

I did not see her again for forty years. She looked me up and we had lunch in New York. The years had creased our faces, filled out our bodies and made them lumpy, done something odd to our teeth. She had had two bad divorces, had two grown, married children of whom she was ferociously proud, she said, though they hadn't done anything in particular (the boy was a banker, the girl a physiotherapist). Becky had read two of my gay novels, she admitted. Now at least, I thought, she knows our romantic fiasco was my fault. Even so, she seemed available, even eager to date me while we were in "the flower of age," as the French refer to people past their sell-by date.

Strange Places

BECAUSE GAY MEN ARE (OR were, in my day) always ready for sex and because a hookup can be swift, encounters can take place anywhere, if the participants are sufficiently motivated. The usual places are gay bathhouses, public toilets (cottaging), parks at night, truck stops; in gay guides these places, if dangerous, used to be labeled in gay guidebooks as AYOR (at your own risk). Some men are excited by dangerous places (danger queens) where they might be discovered or arrested. Recently we were flying back from New Orleans to New York, for example, when the man in the empty row behind us stuck his hand between our seats to catch our attention. When my husband, Michael, curious, stood up and pretended to get something out of the overhead bin, he saw our neighbor stroking an enormous dick. When we arrived at Kennedy, the guy followed Michael into the men's room. Michael gave him our address. He was a regular visitor for a while.

In my early teens I had sex with young dads in station wagons at the edge of Lake Michigan in Evanston, Illinois; the back seats would be crowded with their children's toys. In Cincinnati in my midteens I was picked up by a young redhead drenched in English Leather cologne who drove us out into a remote cornfield. In my twenties I met the only male who danced in a ballet troupe for men in drag; all the other men of this all-male company were in tutus dancing as swans or dead wilis in drag. They called themselves "the world's greatest all-male comic ballet." To make a living when he wasn't performing, this guy lived in a ballet studio, where he was the sporadic super by day and where he lived by night. He was the one to wipe down the mirrors, sweep and straighten everything, restore the practice space to order. He aired it out. It was one floor up and looked out on Bleecker Street near Sullivan. At the time I lived around the corner and would join him at night. There he'd make me coffee on his illegal hot plate. Or pass me a joint. We'd dance in the nude in the dark, or rather he'd dance and I would stumble about, like Bottom pursuing Titania, breathily caressing him across those bare boards in front of those walls of mirrors illuminated just by the distant, feeble streetlights. He was as poetic as the place demanded. He'd take my glasses off and in my shortsighted eyes he'd become just a silvery, moving reflection, a spinning, stretching presence, a warm breath on my nape, warm hands at my waist, his lean, handsome face just a pale streak in motion.

He had a sense of occasion.

He must have been from the West Coast because his was a philosophical turn of mind. He spoke of "transcendence," of "energy," and of "vibes." Maybe he had Bell's palsy because his face was frozen on one side, which made his utterances all the more oracular. I think he got tired of me. Each time I buzzed I would wait a while until eventually he would tell me over the intercom that he was busy. I finally got the idea. Maybe he was used to penetrating lither, more agile men. Or maybe he was used to New Age exchanges with men who wanted wisdom and not just sex, who were eager to learn new yoga poses or to discuss how you are what you eat. Or how to transmit thoughts. How to sort out their chakras. How and when to drink your own urine (or your mentor's). Anyway I was just a sex hound and not an adept, a clumsy slut, not a disciple. Some nights I'd look up and see the overhead spotlights switched off and the practice room plunged into darkness and I'd wonder whom the lucky man the dancer-janitor was partnering or instructing tonight or sweeping . . . off his feet.

* * *

I LIKED PUBLIC BATHROOMS. BEHIND Notre Dame or to one side of Washington Square. In the old days, the men's rooms on the subways were still in use (now they're all padlocked shut, though I've heard some are opening again). When you'd drop your dime in the door and enter, everyone would pull apart. But when they'd see you were in on the game, too, they'd go back to their debauches. A young, hung boy would have half a dozen men leeching on him, one at each armpit, one licking his butt, two competing for his cock, yet another French-kissing him. Guys standing at urinals would be checking each other out. Guys in coat and tie, before they rushed home on the way back from the office, would be roosting on toilets, right on the ceramic bowls without plastic seats or wooden doors, eager to blow someone, anyone, afraid of plain-clothesmen, who were identifiable by their unornamented big black lace-up shoes. They were called the "pretty policemen" and were chosen for their youth and beauty; they were skilled at entrapment and arrest.

Public toilets at suburban commuter train stations were the worst, since the guileless if horny married men weren't on the qui vive and were easily entrapped—and then their names and faces were published on the front page of the community paper, the *Southampton Gazette* as it were, for their kids and neighbors and local service people to see. Same-sex scandals were considered much worse than bankruptcy, alcoholism, domestic abuse, or heterosexual peccadilloes and were rivaled in awfulness only by being identified as a Communist or heroin addict. Most suburban marriages of couples over forty, I'm told, are sexless, but how humiliating to have your husband or father identified as a homosexual, as a sex pig at that and not even one of those sensitive, tormented, and hopefully suicidal gays who only imagined their perversions, like those redeemable characters in "problem plays" who, if they didn't off themselves, were saved for normality by the kindly mothers of their best friends.

Whereas heterosexual men worry about impotence, and castration is their greatest fear, gays always have other sex organs—their holes, their mouths, their hands, their dildos, their whips. As in the play *Bent*, in which one prisoner in a death camp talks another to a climax, words are our secret weapons even where touch is forbidden. I like to think some of my books have cost some cum to a few readers. I've seen guys on sex sites looking for someone to castrate them, to help them get rid of their pesky balls so they can live vicariously through their partner's virility. No wonder Mary Renault's *The Persian Boy* attracts so many readers; it is the story of Alexander the Great's love for a castrated teenage boy, the ultimate bottom. On bondage sites there are pictures of a wide range of penis cages to which only the sadistic partner has the key.

Strange places for sex? I lived on the Île Saint-Louis in Paris for many years and I'd cruise the gardens at the end of the island, the opposite end of the one adjoining Notre Dame. I would crouch in the bushes or go down the steps to the quays. Once I was fucked by a young man with a tiny dick and a beautiful body. He was so special I lured him back to my apartment on the nearby rue Poulletier. After a delirious night, I pleaded with him to visit me again. He said, "No, I can't. I'm kept in a big town house in the Marais by a very jealous German baron who has spies following me all the time. Tonight I shook them, I hope, but I must stay faithful to him in my fashion. No repeats with tricks. I love him, I love my life where I do nothing but work out, dine out in three-star restaurants with friends and the baron when he's in Paris. You understand, of course?"

I spent some years in Italy. In Venice the toilets off the Rialto Bridge were cruisy as was what we called the *molo nero*, the dark wharf between the Piazza San Marco and Harry's Bar. In that strip of quay, where newspapers of every language were sold by day from a dozen little green stands, chained shut at night with lowered metal grills, and where the overhead lights had mercifully been extinguished, we would cruise. Never Venetians themselves, since it was such a small town where you were always visible to neighbors because you had to walk beside your new partner, undoubtedly a foreigner whom no one knew, or stand beside him on a vaporetto, a public transportation boat. Life was lived in public in Venice. If you were ill, for instance, dying or dead, your body had to be carried through the *calle* to a waiting boat from *pronto seccorso*, first aid. There were no secrets in Venice, though foreigners thought of it as mysterious, especially with its heavy fogs and sparse population in winter.

I lived in the spectacular fifteenth-century Palazzo Barbaro and lured several guys (all foreigners) back to my floor. Not strange, perhaps, but historic, filled with ghosts. The painted library had been Henry James's bedroom (there are even photos of his small metal bed, which looks like a torture machine placed on the vast marble floor) and the kitchen had been Sargent's studio when he was painting the American proprietors, the Curtis family, in the *salotto* of the piano nobile. Incidentally, the exterior of the palace was the model for Isabella Stewart Gardner's museum in Boston. I remember once bringing back from the *molo nero* to the palace a famous German Catholic novelist who had a dick as big as a child's arm and a bespectacled sweet face like Schubert's. Years later, when I interviewed a German woman, a sculptor, I uttered his name without mentioning the context. She laughed and said he had been her lover. "There's one who never touched a man. He's one for our side," she said in her good-natured, sophisticated way. I didn't dare to contradict her. Google tells me he's ten years younger than I, and he's written many books inspired by his morality and won every important literary prize. I notice he's never married.

In 1970, when I was thirty, I lived in Rome for half a year and had many nocturnal adventures in the Colosseum, which in those days was open to anyone day and night and was a major cruising spot. I had a regular there, a Romanian with a normal body but the voice of a young girl. His Italian was as limited as mine, though Italian was the only language we had in common. The next year I was exploring the newfangled back rooms in New York, dark spaces in bars where people had sex or met casual partners. The rooms had just come into existence in the post-Stonewall era. There I saw a dishy couple who were looking for a third but no matter how often I spread my wings they took no interest in me. Then I saw my Romanian friend from the Colosseum and started chattering with him in Italian. Suddenly the couple were interested in me because I was exotic. They approached me cautiously and asked, "Do. You. Speak. English?"

I replied, "A leetle beet," and went home with them and kept up my broken English all night.

In back rooms people were absolutely uninhibited. I once saw a guy watching a couple where the top was really hung. The spectator pulled the bottom off the cock forcefully and with a sigh of pleasure planted it in his own bum. In Paris, back rooms were ideal since the French can't speak to someone without an introduction but they can grope a complete stranger in a back room, where normal etiquette is suspended.

When I lived in Paris, I spent several summers in Istanbul on the wonderful island called Büyükada, a retreat half an hour from the city by hydroplane. It was where the Byzantine princes would be exiled by their brother the emperor. Its lush estates, big houses, and countless yachts are on an island where cars are forbidden and the only transportation is horses and carriages; Büyükada is Turkey's Mackinac Island but much larger and more glamorous and has the advantage of being so close to a magical city by *hydroglisseur.* Most of the workers on the island are Kurds. The sailors on the yachts are Kurdish and they have potluck dinners on one boat or another. I was invited to one of those meals. Everyone ate fast without conversation then lit cigarettes, sat back, and, through the one guy who spoke English, pelted me with questions. Which religion was the true one, Islam or Christianity? Were Americans aware of the Kurds' plight? Did I think Allah rewards the virtuous with riches and power?

I told them I was an atheist, which made them all laugh incredulously, and that half of the Americans were nonbelievers but that many of us had an immense respect for Islam and thought of the Prophet as one of the wisest men who ever lived. I told them (it was the mideighties) few Americans had ever heard of the Kurds or would be able to locate Turkey on a map. I said that only one-third of the Americans had passports. Twelve percent of the American population lived below the poverty line; many of these went to bed hungry every night. How could this be, they asked, since America was the richest country in the world? I said, "Some Americans are very rich and some very poor."

They laughed and said, "Like Turkey."

I had a very boyish lover at the time and one night, when we were heading home, the Kurdish supervisor of a building site gave me a red rose and my partner a pink rose. Later, standing among the girders of the new house, which smelled of sap, I gave the Kurd a blow job.

In town on the main upscale shopping street, İstiklal Caddesi, I caught the eye of a tall, lanky teen in the crowd of pedestrians. The poet James Merrill had taught me to point at my victim then myself and then rub two fingers together (in Greece it would be "You, me, *paréa* [party]?"). I thought I'd try the finger game here in Turkey with him and he laughed and joined me. Looking up every word painfully in my Turkish-English dictionary, I told him that I'd be living on Büyükada in July and he should meet me at the embarcadero there on July 1 exactly at noon. Though that was six months later he kept our rendezvous. My boyish American lover called him my Daily Ekmek, the Turkish word for "bread." Ekmek sealed every window shut with closed blinds and curtains. I suppose what we were doing was technically a crime in Turkey. The first time I met him, I urged him to take a bath, which made him laugh. Thanks to the dictionary I found out his family dealt in scrap metal and that they lived on a pile of recuperated brass and steel; every time after that he was clean and well-dressed, thanks to the money I slipped him, I guess. I remember when a Turkish woman arranged a rental on Büyükada, she said she'd had to lie to the proprietor that my wife and children would be joining me later. Single men of my age (forty) were suspect in Turkey. I invited additional (free) lovers from England and America, even France.

In New York in the seventies we would have orgies in the holds of empty trucks parked at the foot of Christopher Street under the abandoned railroad tracks that are now the High Line. Or just as often in the abandoned warehouses lining the Hudson River and protruding out into it. The first chapter of my early novel *Nocturnes for the King of Naples* is a sort of poetic re-creation of that milieu. I lived nearby on Horatio near West Street. I don't think I courted danger; it didn't excite me. But because gay sex flourished in these terrae incognitae, I came to associate them with wild, unrelenting sex. I thought it was quite normal to take a break from writing at two in the morning, saunter down to the piers, and have sex with twenty men in a truck. I remember when I wrote that I'd had sex over the years with three thousand men, one of my contemporaries asked pityingly, "Why so few?"

The Kabuki

When I was just fourteen or fifteen, I went to see the Kabuki, traditional Japanese dance theater, in Chicago, the first time the art had come to America. I went with my mother's then boyfriend, Mr. Hamilton, and his handsome eighteen-year-old son, Bob. I was seated next to Bob, who'd just spent the summer doing construction work and had the tan and muscles to show for it.

Later I learned that the American occupation government under General MacArthur had wanted to ban the Kabuki altogether because it supposedly promoted traditional values, which the Americans were intent on uprooting (militarism, emperor worship, Shinto, feudalism, and so on) and replacing with baseball and democracy. Faubion Bowers, the MacArthur aide-de-camp who had translated from English to Japanese and back again during the historic meeting between Hirohito and MacArthur, had defended the Kabuki as a great world art form and convinced MacArthur to let it survive and even send it on tour to American cities. Bowers, reputedly, was gay, one of the several young American officers who idolized MacArthur, knew Japanese, and revered the Japanese arts (Bowers wrote a first book on ukiyo-e prints, a book I read as a teen). Though Bowers was married for a while and even produced a playboy son, it seems he preferred men and late in life even worked with a friend of mine on an AIDS hotline back here in the States. The female roles in Kabuki, as in plays in Shakespeare's time, were all played by males; apparently those Japanese boys were often rent boys, which led to the theater being located outside the city limits of Tokyo (or Edo, as it was known then). This queer association retrospectively consecrated my own adventure. Years later I read *The Great Mirror of Male Love*, written in the seventeenth century, in which I discovered that the keenest practitioners of boy love were samurai and Buddhist priests, despite their vows of chastity.

Thanks to Bowers (who'd arranged for a successful performance of Kabuki for the American army) we were seeing this "exotic" form of theater, though without the difficult plots and all-day staging of scenes from various plays, during which Japanese audiences would picnic, doze, and chatter. No dozing for us, just stylized dance and falling cherry blossoms.

Relentlessly horny, I pressed my calf experimentally against Bob's. As a caddy I'd tried this technique on another caddy as we waited on a bench. He loudly denounced me: "What are you, some sort of Liberace?" But instead of shifting away, Bob pressed back. By the time of the intermission, when our parents toddled off for their highballs, we were both erect and chose to wait in our seats. During intermission we made a plan to get together. We had a television at a time when they were still fairly rare. Bob said he'd come over next Friday evening to watch his favorite, the crooner Perry Como. Then he'd drink so many beers he'd tell my mother he was too drunk to drive home and ask her if he could stay over. I had twin beds in my room and she assigned one to Bob. A second after lights out we'd thrown the sheets back and I pounced on him, in awe of his magnificent male muscles. I don't think I'd ever been to bed with such a bronzed muscleman, who smelled delightfully of beer and Camels, who would French-kiss me, who gave me free rein over his warm body, the sort of built-up body few American men in that era possessed. Think of Jimmy Stewart's unprepossessing chest in Hitchcock's 1954 mystery thriller, *Rear Window.* Grace Kelly was the most beautiful woman in the world and one felt she could desire poor pale, flabby Stewart only out of the goodness of her heart.

Men became sex objects only in the eighties, though Brando had pointed the way years earlier. Americans felt queasy discussing the male body. The face, possibly, since God had invented that. But the body made everyone uncomfortable; even in gay-oriented homo physique magazines the bodies were just an afterthought, a way of connecting the beautiful face to the overflowing nut sack or powerful buttocks. For me it was a religious experience to touch this god, kiss him, hold him in my feeble filiform arms, these useless pale appendages. I was so exultant about being initiated into this ancient cult, these Eleusinian mysteries, that I came out to my mother a month later. In her slow, deliberate, "sensitive" way, while she was washing dishes and I was drying, she said, "Dear, I'm thinking of marrying Mr. Hamilton."

"Then," I shot back, "it will have to be a double wedding since Bob and I are lovers." I'd been reading Oscar Wilde.

I can't imagine what I was thinking with my outrageous remark. This was the fifties, after all. My mother phoned Bob and in a voice shaking with rage asked him how he'd dared to "take advantage" of her child. She didn't denounce him to his father, luckily, but there were no more Perry Como evenings for me.

Fifty years later Bob looked me up in Paris and as two late-middle-aged men we had a rematch in bed. We'd both lost our looks by then, but I found the moment moving. He'd become a sports doctor for a Catholic boys' school and spent his days massaging the bruises and cramps of teen athletes. He told me he'd made good investments over the years and earned several million dollars. He'd always been embarrassed by his father's relative poverty as a journalist. When Bob died a couple years after that, I discovered he'd left his fortune to the Catholic Church—in gratitude, I suppose, for working with all those fine young athletes.

People assume the Eisenhower years in the Midwest were colorless, tone-deaf, uneventful. I suppose I could have been born in another country to another family, been a viscount and gone to Eton and Oxford, my family might have owned a castle and a Rubens, but even in my humble Illinois suburb, I was at a strange "inflection point," as people say now, between fearless, overweening homosexual lust, Kabuki, the trials and wit of Oscar Wilde, the overexcited imagination of a moviegoer, the buried guilt and exaltation of my "white trash" Protestant forebears, condemned to hell and then mysteriously "saved" over the weekend at a camp meeting. Those were strange days, when museums were empty, tourism had not yet become the number one industry in the world, most Americans were deferential and uninvolved in politics, when the rich and famous were remote and had been knighted by God and were not the cause of resentment, a time when the three greatest public evils were Communism, heroin addiction, and homosexuality.

Poison Ivy

IN THE 1970S GAY MEN in Manhattan would haunt the baths. There were several saunas, to suit different tastes. In the basement of the Ansonia, a belle époque Upper West Side apartment building, where Toscanini had lived, there were the Continental Baths, entirely restored with a big clean gushing swimming pool next to a performance space where Bette Midler and Barry Manilow got their start. Hip young heterosexual couples, dressed up, would come in for the midnight show while gay boys, wrapped in towels with naked chests, stood around on the edges, half paying attention and half cruising. If a heavy cruise produced a tumescence in a towel, that could be taken care of in a nearby maze, shielded from the straight visitors' gaze. The bodies were typical of the 1970s—slender, hairless, toned but not muscular. I always resented the acts; I didn't want all these clothed breeders profaning the temple, nor did I want the boys in towels distracted from the business at hand.

Then there were the Everard Baths, in a wasteland between Chelsea and Murray Hill, a foul stew rumored to be owned and operated by the Police Benevolent Association (cops sat around at the entrance). The pool in the basement, always empty, was pocked with islands of scum; a bather thought his leg might be dissolved to the hip if he ventured in. Bare light bulbs in metal cages, cigarette-littered hallways, dimly lit steam rooms full of motionless walruses half-undraped, private rooms with cots covered with bare black fabric that looked as if worn away with vitiligo, the Michael Jackson skin disfigurement.

The crowd was older and heavier. Now that I'm both, I have to admire the persistence of the "trolls"; just when you were kissing a guy your age and touching his erect cock through the towel, a troll would be kneeling in the old, cold come beside you both and begging for dick. It wasn't a scenario I liked, but sometimes it would happen: he'd jerk you off and suck your partner to completion while you two youngsters were romancing with soul kisses above the gristle.

In May 1977 nine men died in a fire that destroyed the top two floors of the Everard, but the floors were quickly rebuilt. The Everard wouldn't permanently close until 1986, when AIDS was burning through the gay population, closed by the closeted Mayor Ed Koch.

Another bath in the lower teens near Sixth Avenue, Man's Country, was theatrical with its prison cells and, on a higher floor, a fake truck with glowing headlights and barred face and an interior hold for having sex—a re-creation of the busier but more dangerous real trucks at the foot of Christopher Street, full of pickpockets (there were no pockets on the wraparound towels in the sauna). The whole setup seemed so camp it made a deflating mockery of our transgressive scenarios (become a prisoner in a safe environment or suck cock in the back of a scrubbed, air-conditioned truck). It was as if a jungle tiger with a bloody mouth were changed into Hello Kitty, paws up.

In one of these baths I met a fierce young man with a beard and hollowed-out eyes who would barge into my room, where I was lying placidly on my stomach, feeling neglected though I'd already attracted four "customers." He was as courtly as a pneumatic drill, as smooth as 220-grit sandpaper, and yet there was something of the demon lover in his unrelenting ardor. Most men posing as tops seemed to be fundamentally bottoms ("Today's trade is tomorrow's competition," in the queens' vernacular). But this guy seemed almost driven to be inside me, never so happy as when he was penetrating me; he urged himself on to go deeper and deeper, harder and harder. I was equally voracious, stimulated by his brutishness. We were in a fever clinic of reciprocal desire. For a while I would see him only at the baths. Once he saw me, he was sure to come in without hesitation; he could have no doubt as to our compatibility or our urgency.

Once I saw him taking a cigarette break with another guy, his legs draped cozily over the guy's lap. Oh, I thought, a lover.

Which was right, in a way, but as it turned out, they were both aggressive in bed, in love but unsuited, reduced to a friendship that Howard Moss, the poet, would have described as "old, familiar and inadequate." I can't remember how I broached the subject with the friend, but the postcoital, backstage intervals at the baths can be chummy and maybe we started talking about my satyr in the canteen over a Diet Coke. He told me that they'd been "together" for twelve years, ever since university in Lawrence, Kansas, but their love for each other (they lived together and worked together at a small shop editing commercials) was real but frustrating since they were both "pitchers" and neither could tolerate being a "catcher." Of course it was a dilemma that excited me.

The satyr invited me to their house and impaled me as if he were a warrior-priest and I an unstoppable vampire. Why are these neural traces from fifty years ago still inscribed somewhere in the hippocampus? Probably because I've revisited them so often in the intervening years. An essential part of memory is called rehearsal—the more you revisit a memory the longer it sticks.

I was going to move to San Francisco for work the Monday after a weekend in the Pines on Fire Island when

I spotted my satyr at a bar. It was a moonlit, sultry, late-August night. I was heading home but aware that he was following me. Suddenly he grabbed me from behind then circled around and began to kiss me with his usual passion. In a few moments, ignoring the rare passersby, he had clawed off my shorts and was fucking me. We had soon fallen off the boardwalk and were rolling in the weeds. By the time I got out to San Francisco I was covered with poison ivy, deep red welts. They must not have had it out there because the doctor had no idea how to soothe my inflamed skin. I think we settled on calamine lotion.

I saw the satyr only once again. After my San Francisco job blew up a year later (the magazine went broke), I headed back for New York. Out there I hadn't really known how to "score," as gays said then, imitating heroin addicts. I didn't have a car. I didn't fancy being fisted. Everyone seemed to be in bed by ten and ready to greet the dawn with finger bells and cosmic assurance.

New York felt as comfortable as an old pair of loafers. I headed to the baths and I saw him in a room. He was gaunt and his eyes were ringed and protruding. We were thirty and he looked as if he were dying. He just waved feebly in my direction. He probably was dying.

I keep reading François Villon, who may have lived in the fifteenth century but could have been speaking for us:

> Where are those gracious gallants now,
> whom I ran with in those long-gone times,

such sweet singers, such good talkers,
so pleasing to all in word and deed?
Some are dead and stiff already;
of these, there's simply nothing left.
May they find their peace in Paradise,
and God save those of us still left!

Stonewall

I WAS ACTUALLY AT THE Stonewall Riots fifty years ago, the beginning of the current Gay Rights movement. Not because I was a radical. Quite the contrary. As a middle-class white twenty-nine-year-old who'd been in therapy for years trying to go straight, I was initially disturbed by seeing all these Black and brown people resisting the police. I had at one time been a regular patron of this Greenwich Village bar, but in recent months the crowd had changed to kids mainly from Harlem, many in drag.

In the early sixties Mayor Wagner had closed down all gay and lesbian bars in a misguided effort to "clean up" the city for tourists visiting the World's Fair. But by 1969 those days seemed long gone. We had a new mayor, John Lindsay, who looked like a Kennedy and we assumed was liberal. We gays weren't in a good mood. Judy Garland (the equivalent of Lady Gaga or Taylor Swift today) had just died and was lying in state in a funeral home on the Upper West Side. It was very, very hot and everyone was sitting out on stoops. And then this! A crowded gay bar had just been raided, a reminder of recent persecution.

Whereas gays had always run away in the past, afraid of being arrested and jailed, these Stonewall African Americans and Puerto Ricans and drag queens weren't so easily intimidated. They were used to fighting the police. They lit fires, turned over cars, and mocked the cops, even battering the heavy Stonewall doors where some policemen were retaining members of the staff and customers, waiting for the paddy wagon to return.

The protests went on for three days and the whole area around Christopher Street and Seventh Avenue was cordoned off. Ours may have been the first funny revolution. When someone shouted "Gay is good" in imitation of "Black is beautiful," we all laughed; at that moment we went from seeing ourselves as a mental illness to thinking we were a minority. Certainly the era was rich in rebellion—the protests against the Vietnam War, the Black Power movement, and the Women's movement. We'd all seen on TV men burning their draft cards, athletes making the Black Power salute, radical women such as the Redstockings being "intolerable" (a slogan). Now a chorus line of gay boys came out kicking behind the cops shouting, "We are the Pink Panthers." In those days there was a women's prison (since razed) on the corner of Greenwich Avenue and Christopher Street. Soon the women were shouting down encouragement from their cells and strumming their metal cups against the bars.

Although I'd been shocked at first by these exuberant actions, soon I felt exhilarated by the expression of the indignation I'd repressed for so long. I was joining in, despite my years of submission. Like most revolutions, the occasion for this one was ill chosen. When the Bastille was stormed, there were only six pampered aristocrats in it, one of them the Marquis de Sade, who clearly needed to be locked up. In a similar way, the Stonewall was an unhygienic, exploitative Mafia bar tightly guarded by Mafia henchmen. No matter—the bar may not have been worth defending but the energy of the defense was admirable.

And the energy continued. I moved to Rome for a year but when I came back, dozens of bars and discos had opened, go-go boys were dancing under black light, the back rooms were crowded—and the libertine seventies were being born. I even saw Fellini on a snowy night being led into a Sheridan Square gay bar on a prospecting tour, accompanied by Stan's old college roommate, the one who'd been so mean to his chauffeur. We were trendy!

Gay studies started. Gay politics were being nurtured by new groups, one more radical than the next. I started attending Maoist consciousness-raising groups in which no one was permitted to challenge anyone else. By the end of the decade I was a member of a writers' group, facetiously named the Violet Quill. No one wanted to imitate straight life; we were against "assimilation."

Then in 1981 the AIDS era ended the party. Gay cruises and resorts went bankrupt. Hospitals were overwhelmed with the ill and dying. I was one of the six founders of the Gay Men's Health Crisis. Hundreds of our friends and acquaintances and celebrities died. As the writer Fran Lebowitz pointed out, not only did gay creative people die but so did their gay audiences, those cultivated men who'd been the consumers of high culture. Suddenly everyone wanted to look healthy; going to the gym replaced going to the opera.

★ ★ ★

WHEREAS ONE CAN COMPLAIN TODAY that Pride parades are corporate sponsored and gay marriage is heteronormative and that gay culture has become commercial, that dismissive point of view toward the liberation movement can be arrogant and unfeeling. It ignores how many people still suffer from oppression due to religious fundamentalism. American fundamentalists have influenced Ugandans to pass Kill the Gays legislation. Every year scores of homosexuals are executed in Muslim countries or, in America, commit suicide out of fear and low self-esteem. More than half the teens who kill themselves are gay. In Western Europe and the Americas gay couples are allowed to marry or at least declare themselves joined by a bond.

Some people romanticize the pre-Stonewall period, but in truth there was a high rate of alcoholism among gays then, it was rare to meet a committed gay couple, no gay I knew had children, few gays had splendid careers, many were in therapy trying to go straight—there's a whole litany of gay deprivations from the pre-Stonewall years. Most of us devoted all of our energy merely to being gay. It wasn't something you could assume and just get on with your life. Employers were suspicious of or revolted by gays except in a few industries (hairdressing, for instance, or interior decoration). My father would fire an employee because he was thirty and suspiciously unmarried.

The first group to benefit from the freedoms won fifty years ago were white men; now the struggle continues among lesbians, people of color, the trans population—and all those living under dangerously right-wing, hostile religious regimes. In a sense this return to gender-fluid people and gay and lesbian people of color is a recapitulation of the original Stonewall warriors, those drag queens and tough kids from Harlem. They have given new life to a movement, Pride, that in big-city America at least had become corporate, uninspired, and materialistic.

I suppose most people imagine that someone such as me who has had sex with thousands of people must have been doing it by rote, must have been mechanical and coldly indifferent to everything but his very private, intimate sensations. But in truth my gay life in my twenties was exhausting. I had to invent for my relatives and colleagues heterosexual partners for myself that no one ever met and to *remember* all my lies.

In my late twenties I had a Mormon sort of fantasy that I could choose a man as long as I was still attractive (under thirty-five?) and we'd be "sealed" for all eternity in an exclusive, unremitting love almost as if we were committed to a spaceship not destined to land for thousands of years. On YouTube you can see a Mormon sealing ceremony, the groom with a sort of white turban, the bride in a white veil; they're facing each other over a low narrow altar. The bishop, after giving boring love and sex fidelity advice, starts to crack jokes then does the "sealing." I think family members are also sealed together in a different ceremony; I learned about that from a gay youngster who'd been exiled from his disapproving family for all eternity because he'd confessed he was queer; he would be wandering alone around space forever like some lost asteroid. He'd been in the family bubble, then pushed out for his "morals." Good riddance, we'd say, but many Mormon kids kill themselves, alone and freezing in the darkness. Every bit of their future was erased, every giggly ride through the hill country, the unfolding landscape triggering more and more sing-along hymns and group ballads—that was silenced. No lap to sprawl on, no mother's hands with their colorless, trimmed nails to pull an unwanted thread from an old scarf, no heartening wink over a bad report card.

I was always inclined toward love. If someone would respond to me, open up his body to me, smear kisses across my bruised lips, I would instantly begin to love him, to imagine our future, plan to prepare his favorite dishes, find his points of secret vanity and play up to them.

When I drank (too much), I'd fall for bartenders. They are perfect objects of lust—usually handsome, virile, speedy, friendly for tips—looking more and more active and crisp as you, the drinker, become more and more sodden. The problem for bartenders—hot ones in a New York gay bar—is that they have too many temptations and don't get off until four in the morning. By that time I'd be blubbering with desire and drink: a mess. Since 1983 I haven't had a drink and therefore I always now run out of energy by midnight and time has become a glue trap.

I seldom thought the way women in the past thought about love—that their mate should be a good provider, a family man, religious, solid, faithful, high in status but basically a good guy, not so high he might tempt another woman to "cheat" with him or run off with him. I joke about being a "material girl," but I've only ever seen a man's wealth as an unexpected benefit, something far from essential, even embarrassing. No, I go for the real solid virtues: big dick, a top in bed, beautiful body, someone frequently stoned, jealous and possessive until the day he drops you and becomes jealous over someone new. A job is just a refractory period between orgasms; socializing is just a tease, a delay before serious fucking.

Despite my frivolous tone, I recognize that Stonewall inaugurated an epoch when partners of the same sex could claim, maybe for the first time in history, their common humanity, their dignity, their rights. This victory permitted us to put our creative energies into something other than simply enduring. We could build our marriages, love our families, invest ourselves into our work, express ourselves in uncoded novels and poems and in the thousand other endeavors created by human ingenuity. This freedom is something we will never relinquish.

Sadomasochism

LONG AGO SUSAN SONTAG WROTE an influential essay, "Fascinating Fascism," in which she conflated the modern leather scene with historical fascism: in pornographic literature, films, and gadgetry throughout the world, especially in the United States, England, France, Japan, Scandinavia, Holland, and Germany, the SS has become a referent of sexual adventurism. Much of the imagery of far-out sex has been placed under the sign of Nazism. Boots, leather, chains, Iron Crosses on gleaming torsos, swastikas, along with meat hooks and heavy motorcycles, have become the secret and most lucrative paraphernalia of eroticism. In the sex shops, the baths, the leather bars, the brothels, people are dragging out their gear. But why? Why has Nazi Germany, which was a sexually repressive society, become erotic? How could a regime that persecuted homosexuals become a gay turn-on?

When Susan wrote "Fascinating Fascism," I took exception to her argument and I still do. I thought S&M was fascinating to everyone. I remember a shrink of the time studied the fantasies of gay men and found they were often about submission even if they usually didn't act on them. He was a good enough scientist to do the same study of straight people—with the same results! I heard a comedian the other night say he wanted to become gay just to rile his neighbor who thought gays were perverted. "So are straights," the comedian said, "if they're doing it right."

I think that S&M was also coherent with the clone movement of the 1970s, when gay men tried to redefine themselves as no longer limp-wristed lispers but as muscle-Mary machos. Under the influence of Guattari and Deleuze, I wrote in the 1970s a complicated, probably misguided essay in the *New Masses* about S&M as a form of pleasure and as a way of dramatizing class conflict. I wonder. . . . I read a study of gay leather guys that said they were vegetarians (pace Hitler), against the death penalty, sensitive to the sight of physical pain. I've wasted hours trying to track down these sources. Leo Bersani thought as babies we were converted to masochism because we need to eroticize the helplessness we're feeling in order to deal with it. We need to desire feeling helpless. Something like Freud's repetition compulsion in which a child in her play repeats painful experiences (with her mother doll, say, spanking her daughter doll) in order to gain mastery over the hurt.

In any event I never noticed much SS regalia. And as Jean Genet contended, he who was a leftist anarchist but found the Nazis sexy, erotic tastes are seldom coherent with political opinions. Only Americans think your fantasies can invalidate your sympathies and ideas.

Rather than the Nazis, the gay leather scene is far more detailed. Here's a typical posting:

> TPE, slave training, bootlicking, spit, chastity, domestic service, humiliation, urinal service, ashtray service, rimming, feet, sounding, electro, impact play, and hole work and service (along with much more).

TPE is "total power exchange," i.e., the bottom gives up entirely and surrenders to the will of the top. Chastity is wearing a cage over your junk that keeps you from cumming; your master has the only key. Sounding is inserting a glass rod into your urethra. Impact play is hitting. *Not a single Iron Cross in the mix.*

I first discovered my sadism when I was in my mid-twenties and tricked with a small guy who kept saying, "Don't touch my hair. I told you, don't touch my hair." Though he was a bottom he had so many irritating rules I finally slapped his ass and he came. I was shocked that I was capable of that, even more shocked that he'd deliberately been needling me into a rage, and most surprised that my anger flipped his switch. That was my introduction to what the French, using the English word, call *hard* sex without pronouncing the initial *h*.

My rage was spontaneous, not premeditated. I could label it as sadism only slowly and in retrospect. My image of myself is that I am kind and pacifying. Never choleric. As it was, I rather gloried in my aggressiveness. But would I have if my partner hadn't liked it? If he'd furiously rejected it, would I have felt repentant?

Deleuze has argued that masochism is not the twin of sadism but has an entirely different etiology. I guess I disagree with him, at least in my own case. Although maybe I became a conscious sexual masochist only as I got older, even old and jaded, I was always a psychological masochist, invariably unhappy in love. I've argued that we suffer not because we want to suffer but because we want something else that always causes suffering, something such as love from someone too beautiful to be accessible, or fidelity from someone promiscuous by nature, or love from someone who is young and has so many problems that the last thing he wants or needs is a serious love affair. Men in their forties, say, who have a career and friends and know who they are—they're the ones looking for a great love, the cherry on top of the sundae. Whereas men in their twenties are still struggling with coming out and feel frustrated and friendless and all they want is a fun, glamorous crowd, not a needy middle-aged lover, someone basking in worldly success but wanting only an idealized young partner. As a pre-Stonewall gay I needed years and years to feel comfortable being homosexual, then as a late-blooming writer I was never secure about my position in the world, my reputation, or (with good reason) my earning power.

I met a sweet but tiresome slave in the 1970s in New York. He was a smiling guy who introduced me to Linda Ronstadt and Anne Rice. He read all of *Interview with the Vampire* out loud to me. He made his living selling greeting cards from door-to-door—which may have accounted for his eternal grin, the salesman's brave smile in the face of hostile strangers. Nothing could faze him. He was from Kentucky, from the usual fundamentalist family, who had disowned him for the usual reason—being gay. He always made a neat appearance with his "What, me?" insouciance. He was impeccably showered and douched. In those pre-app days, you could discover your partner's sexual tastes only gradually, experimentally, by judging when they groaned with pleasure after you'd uttered some threat or touched some vulnerable, pre-eroticized part of the body (a swollen nipple, say, a gaping hole, a Prince Albert—i.e., a silver cleat stapled through the foreskin).

Since it was all make-believe for me, I felt obliged to be stoic and silent. The silence part didn't suit me and meant I had to listen to hours of Linda Ronstadt and Anne Rice (both of whom I admire but wouldn't put at the top of any list). My slave never drew a breath and, like his mother, no doubt, found everything and everyone "cute" or "precious." New York, with its intellectual pretensions and career tensions, didn't reward my friend in the ways his sweetness and naïveté deserved; I suppose he was in it for the physical abuse. I never knew someone so interested in his own life.

My abuse was more verbal. I would tell him what tortures I was going to inflict on him (seldom executed beyond a cheek-reddening spanking). He was almost inert. Nor did he get an erection or jerk off. Sometimes we'd go out for a meal afterward, during which he would chatter about what he'd discovered about Linda Ronstadt's life and how Anne Rice lived in an abandoned monastery in New Orleans and had become obsessed with blood because she'd had a hemophiliac child (I never verified those facts). I would sit there lugubriously, playing my silent, tough-guy role, feeling tortured by so much motor mouthing. He didn't seem to know I was a writer (nor was I much of one in those days). He drank a lot of beer. He'd also have to drink my piss. He was slender and long waisted but not at all muscular. He didn't exercise, except his jaw. He stopped his Kentucky chatter, at least, while performing the awe-inspiring act of crouching and swallowing my recycled beer. That was a frequent practice in those days; I can remember picking up someone with a yellow handkerchief in the back left pocket of his jeans, indicative of his desires and practices, buying a six-pack, and going into a quiet empty warehouse and recycling our beer for a happy, infantile hour. The beer was warmer, more fragrant, when drunk directly from the tap of my date's microbrewery.

I thought it would be a bonus if I lined up a bigger and realer sadist for Kentucky. My neighbor was a six-foot, four-inch Florida blond, who was featured in a gay pamphlet about the New Macho Gay. He was a huge bodybuilder and ate two or three rotisserie chickens a day, belched a lot, but had lovely old-fashioned manners (he was a leather buddy of the great English poet Thom Gunn). He had grown up with a psycho father who'd been a football star then lost his legs in a drunken car accident and sat in bed all day drinking and ridiculing his sissy son. By the time I knew the Florida blond he'd turned himself into a real man's man, if that's the phrase for a butch homosexual, a builder and a real estate mogul. He liked to sit on my face while jerking off.

I guess Norm (the Floridian) didn't want to tip off his lover that he was up to no good, so he arrived with his leathers in a paper bag. I buzzed him in, and with much clanking and creaking (no Velcro), he donned his chaps and leather jacket. I kept my slave naked, kneeling and blindfolded as we both listened to Norm's backstage costume change. At last he emerged in his chaps but with his crotch and butt naked. When he was half-hard ("a Hollywood loaf"), I removed the blindfold. The leather cap with a visor that threw his face into shadow, the bare, muscular torso under the open leather jacket, the big tumescence in its nest of blond pubes (like the Christ Child in its hay crèche), the pitiless boots, the smell of sweat and leather—all excited me, but the slave just took it as his due, as his unappetizing daily rations, even when Norm found some reason to turn and expose his big, edible butt, which I knew from experience was bliss to chow down on.

My slave seemed unaware of what a wonderful treat I was serving him. His lack of enthusiasm dismayed me and I almost apologized to Norm for my slave's indifference, like that of a Pavlovian dog who refuses to salivate no matter how cunningly he's electrocuted. In his listless, shambling way he backed up on Norm's dick. He who was so voluble backstage was regrettably mute when "on."

I took him to Key West on holiday. After stoically listening to hours of his babble, I realized with a jolt that I didn't like him, that I was punishing him for boring me, not because I lovingly wanted to flog him into excitement. That was a terrible realization, that my hostility was fueled by unmediated scorn not out of a shared and generous taste for torture as a game. Oh, dear, I thought primly, I'm a wicked esthete. Even Sade was a better man—he at least had a genuine and creative hunger for inventing new forms of pain for his lovely, helpless victims.

I wasn't able to look into the polluted depths of my perfidious ennui until we dropped some acid. In the sudden clarity of LSD, as we wandered down the street—lined with bushes whose leaves were made of shiny oilcloth and where the bougainvillea blossoms were fantastic twists of pink crepe paper—I saw a toy car pull up beside me at a red light and I reached in the open window to touch a toy child and the mother began to scream.

And I realized I'd broken all boundaries in my little life, that I'd defiled a stranger and treated a slave heartlessly. My slave was white and had submitted voluntarily, but in my moral crisis I suddenly thought of my slaveholding ancestors in the Confederacy, how my cousin was the notorious racist Strom Thurmond, how my grandfather was a member of the Klan—and I decided then and there to break up with my slave as soon as we returned to New York in three days.

I sought the kindest way to end the affair and decided it was best to lie and pretend that I was a secret slave and had found a wonderful master who had commanded me to fire my own slave, the hillbilly. We had a tearful farewell and he confessed that I didn't really have my heart in my role (which sounds like an exotic sandwich). "What was your clue?" I asked, fearing I'd been insufficiently dominant.

He said, "My previous doms were always warm and loving afterwards, but you never showed the least bit of affection."

⋆ ⋆ ⋆

THE THEME OF THE MASTER turning into someone else's slave got played out twice in my life, alas. Bad karma.

I had a beautiful part-time master; he had a jealous lover but when he was out for a jog, he'd drop in at my place, sweaty and panting from his exercise, and flop across my sunstruck afternoon bed and want to be serviced. He was a writer from the South, obscenely young, who'd come by once for tea and said, "You should go to bed with me; I'm very good sex."

"Ok-k-k . . . ," I stuttered. A perk of being a published writer (the only one).

We both stood up at the same moment and fell into each other's arms. He wrote a play and a professional football player bankrolled it because his sister was acting in it; I knocked myself out inviting the handful of theater critics I knew but none of them felt tempted to review it. I persisted in escorting and dining all these critics even though the writer had recently announced he was leaving me for a scary, formidable sadist. I felt I had to do what I'd promised. When I'd lived in France, the French were always accusing Americans of forgetting their promises; I was determined to prove I was different.

Then on another occasion I fell for a blond painter who worked part-time in a gay bookstore in Los Angeles, where I met him. He had a deep voice, a lean body, and a smile that was like a first prize. He took photos of rather bleak L.A. images (an abandoned supermarket cart under a dying palm tree under a pitiless sun), which he'd then augment by painting certain parts in colorful acrylics. He didn't seem interested in me except as a buddy. I kept inviting him out with Christopher Isherwood and Don Bachardy (writer, painter—get it?) but that didn't lead him toward emulation. We spent a strange New Year's Eve together at a huge L.A. gay sauna. We each went in opposite directions. When we ran into each other again, Keith said, "Just a lot of bottoms on speed."

I thought of writing a gossip column for the *Village Voice* called Bottoms on Speed.

He eventually left me for Mr. Drummer, a sadist icon. But he did send me his little brother, also gay, even sweeter and more handsome, a flight attendant who stayed with me whenever he flew into New York. The brothers were both from Minnesota and had gone with their sister to Norwegian camp in the summers as adolescents; the sister married a Norwegian ice hockey star. I remember calling the younger brother just before he was going to move in and saying neurotically, "This is a bad idea. You'll fall asleep every night and I'll stay awake, crying."

He replied in a fatherly way, "Don't worry. It will all work out," and it did for many years.

My last experience as a sadist was with someone I respected and loved. I was out in California auditioning for a college teaching job I didn't get. I'd been invited by someone from the Classics Department who'd written a book on Ovid's *Heroides* (the versified complaints of women like Ariadne who'd been abandoned by their lovers). Rob had an ingenious, surely incorrect theory about Ovid that he'd blown up into a tenure-track professorship and an eighty-dollar university-press book about how the women were all sort of Asian and the men all sort of European and that expressed world tensions in the classical world (as Jeff Nunokawa, Victorian-literature scholar at Princeton, once said, "To be an academic you just have to have one good idea, which you repeat in six books"). I couldn't figure out why a classicist would be the one to invite me for a reading. The whole three days I was there—driving me around to see the sights, inviting me to a brown-rice sushi restaurant, having me to tea in his exquisite little house—he kept smiling and telling me with his boyish voice and donnish mien what a talent I was! Only when I returned to New York did he phone me to say he'd fallen in love with me.

Exhausted by the six-hour trip, I thought, "Now he tells me," but of course I made plans to return to California right away. He picked me up at the airport and the minute we stepped into his bijou cottage we started kissing. His body didn't feel academic at all but was lithe and vibrant, a pale miracle. I noticed that he let me lead the conversation, although like Susan Sontag (and with even less reason) I like to say I'm a good listener. My nephew, who'd known me when I was young and timid, once said, "You used to listen. Now you interrupt." But Rob wasn't just being polite; he was sending a definite message by being so pliable, physically and conversationally. I tweaked a nipple and he groaned; I put a finger on the entrance to his rectum and he stared at me with the sudden recognition of submission. By the minute he became more and more boyish until soon I had a thirteen-year-old in my arms, not a forty-year-old man.

We never discussed it, but I could sense he was into bondage, even pain, certainly submission. The only thing that confused me was that admiration seemed to be such a determining part of his character; maybe he just admired me and would let me do whatever I wanted, even things he didn't enjoy. I knew from his work on the *Heroides*, however, that he was alive to pre-Christian kink, the most lavish and all-consuming kind, built not on guilt but caprice.

I didn't forget to be tender post coitus this time. His everyday talk was less voluble and more interesting than my previous slave's.

Rob seemed to be obsessed with the woman who lived part-time next door. Marge had many gentlemen callers when she was in residence. She appeared to have money. Though she was fifty or so, she was still a player. She had no interest in her garden whereas my friend was always outdoors hoeing and watering. She never came on to my friend; she was sophisticated and probably knew he was gay. He didn't have many sex adventures to talk about; perhaps chastity was his main vice and I thought of locking his penis in a cage, but it seemed redundant and too much of a commitment on both sides. I would have the only key. What if I didn't want to return to California? What if Rob didn't want me back?

He'd lived in a Carthusian monastery as a graduate student then the Vatican, where everyone spoke Latin. His tutor could translate without pause from *Time* into Latin or from *Vogue Italia*. Rob had a huge vocabulary even for words the Romans had never dreamed of and that he invented on the spot (*faux fur* became *vellus fictus*). *Fashion* was a problem to translate, and yet *synthetic leather* was *saccharums corium*.

On my several trips cross-country I filled my suitcases with black leather ankle straps and a steel rod to keep his legs spread; a gag; handcuffs; nipple clamps; a cat-o'-nine-tails; a ball gag; a box of Godiva chocolates (for the tender aftermath). I was endlessly fascinated by his talk about Ovid and the wronged women of antiquity. Marge seemed a good antidote. She exploited men and wanted nothing from them except a good rogering and a superior bottle of Bordeaux (she herself would supply the wine for the suitably lusty but impecunious young). Somewhere she had a dim static husband like a mossed-over garden god, but he played no part in her life. She gardened men as Alcina did, whereas Rob got plowed but nursed his flowers into bloom in the California sun.

We rendezvoused in northern Italy and went from city to city in a rented car. His parents had been doctors and atheists and he knew nothing about Catholicism. He was shocked by so many paintings of St. Lawrence on the grill, St. Lucy holding her eyes on a tray, St. Catherine's severed head and thumb, or St. Agatha's mammoplasty (her breasts in her hands), and he confessed finally that he couldn't take any more. I protected him from all additional martyrdoms. In Venice we stayed in the Hotel Malibran, which I chose because it was named after a famous opera singer, but the walls were so thin the neighbors complained of Rob's martyrdom. In Rome he took me to the opera and I invited him to a Lucullan feast in a three-star restaurant that had revived ancient Roman recipes (chicken in honey and peppercorns). Although we've always stayed friends, we soon wearied of our sexcesses.

⋆ ⋆ ⋆

MY TWO BEST MASTERS WERE both rent men. One was a handsome nearly square redhead, who was so ridiculously hung that once when my husband walked in on us he couldn't believe such a python existed in unassisted nature. He was a polite, well-spoken man except in the toils of sadism. I asked him when he'd first heard the call (as in call boy), and he said that when he'd first come to New York as a teen, he was so poor he wondered how he'd ever put himself through college. A trick, looking at him in the nude, said, "You've got a million bucks below your belt" (many people used to talk like Damon Runyon characters). While he was still just a kid, he started pole dancing; gays, unlike straight men, are bad tippers for strippers; where a heterosexual man might give ten dollars, a gay man will give one. David, however, would get twenties and forty for a lap dance (in which you can feel him up in a dark booth but not get his cum—except in Montreal, where the stoned teens will cum in your ass for a twenty).

David was very professional but expensive. He would do anything you asked but never reduce his fee of $350, not even for return customers. He was built like a brick outhouse. He would kiss, he would wear my kilt and squat on my face and nearly break my nose, he would indulge in what he called "yellow play" and even "brown play," he would hurt my nipples (the size of pencil erasers), he would obligingly ridicule my tiny penis, he would let me lick his salty, blond axillae. He would crush my head between his *Transformers* biceps and let me tongue his hole. His body was always warm as if he were freshly out of the kiln. His eyes were as blue and white as the Swedish flag. He'd painstakingly lowered his girlish voice like Brahms until it was raucous. His big balls were loose in the sac, stretching out yards of pink flesh, and his dick was large as something that would have saved the lives of three *Titanic* passengers. It looked segmented only because no one could perceive something so long as unified. The head, easily driven out of its camouflage hood, was as wide as a boletus bulb with its eight-centimeter width, its sticky cap, and hidden, sustaining spores.

I'd bought a cheap full-length mirror with a gilt frame for ten dollars on the street, in which David liked to watch himself getting sucked; it looked like something out of an underwater horror movie if I remembered to move my head slightly to one side. The surface of the glass was wavy.

I guess I was like Stan, who thought if his shrinks loved him, they wouldn't charge, and if they didn't love him, what good were they? Of course I realized David was way out of my league. I also knew that it was expensive to maintain such a big body—the extra food, the steroids, the trainer, the gym hours someone had to pay for.

Once I arranged to meet David on Fire Island, where we spent a magical evening hour holding hands beside a bee-loud jasmine bush. We chatted about what we were reading and I kissed his cheek goodbye. He didn't respond, but later he said it was the nicest moment he'd ever spent on the island. I flattered myself that I'd never been to bed with anyone but a thoroughbred, even if I had to pay dear for it; in any event it wasn't true, I who'd once had sex with the village idiot in a public toilet in Caernarfon next to the place where the Prince of Wales was crowned.

⋆ ⋆ ⋆

YIORGOS WAS A HIRED MASTER who was less idyllic. When I met him, he was twenty and wanted to be an opera singer. I knew from my own teenage lessons as an opera singer that no one could tell how your voice would turn out before it was trained (or maybe that's what greedy vocal coaches told the discouraged parents of unpromising students). He never actually sang for me; I guess serious artists don't just sing at the drop of a horned helmet; they need their scales, lemon juice, and warm sprays. His father was Greek and his mother American. They were rich and I have no idea why a scion of the grande bourgeoisie should whore himself out, but even the Empress Messalina was a slut for hire. He had a grand apartment aspirationally near the Metropolitan Opera.

Yiorgos was tall and as beautiful as Michelangelo's *David*, but much better hung with a butt just as chow-downable. He liked wearing my leather vest and steel cock ring and wielding my whip. He was quick to tie a leather string around his immense biceps and wrap a wide leather cuff around his thick wrist. He would probably have used a dildo on me but he must have understood how that would be redundant.

I'd met him on Craigslist, which has now of course gone respectable and canceled its personal ads. After a few visits at my place, I was invited to his, which was grand. He was strangely fussy and insisted on putting down a towel before I sat on his pale leather couch. He didn't want me to moan—the neighbors might hear it, though the walls were thick. If I brought a joint, we would share it; for both of us marijuana didn't have its usual mild, dreamy, giggly effect but instead triggered our most rapacious urges.

Even a sadist can be (should be) courtly and attentive at the beginning and the end, but Yiorgos was as self-centered as the only child of indulgent, enraptured parents could be. Never offered so much as a glass of water, an omission not sadistically intentional but thoughtless. He flicked the whip experimentally, as if rehearsing for real life, forgetting, goddamn it, this was real life. He fell into every mirror as Narcissus drowned in his reflection. If I posed my pier glass against an armchair, he looked at himself, of course, not what I was doing to him. Understandably, people are mean about self-absorbed boys—who are as fragile as they are vain. They know they're loved for their beauty and they know it has an expiration date, but no one can be sure when that day will come, has come.

I invited him to Italy—Rome, Florence, Venice. But he was a strange, infuriating traveling companion. He didn't want me to pay for hotels, nor did he want to pay for them himself. Which meant we had to stay with my friends in each city, which might have seemed an irritating imposition. I'd lived in Rome, spent thirteen summers in Venice, and visited Florence countless times. I broke my own rule that lovers should never travel to cities that one of them knows well and the other has never visited. They should go someplace new to both of them. The know-it-all (usually the older partner) quickly becomes an intolerable bully ("Close your eyes! Close them, goddamn it. Now stand over here. Now you can open them. Isn't that amazing?"), whereas if they're both looking at the Great Buddha of Kamakura for the first time, they can share the experience ("That is soo cool!").

I can't remember where we were in Rome but in Florence we stayed right on the Arno with the super polite

Finzi-Continis. When with my great weight I broke a seventeenth-century chair, the charming wife said, "It's time we got rid of all this old rubbish anyway." When Yiorgos went to see Michelangelo's *David*, I told him that the Baroness von Rezzori could arrange for him to skip the two-hour line, but he said he wanted to stand in the queue so he could talk with all the other young American tourists.

In Venice we stayed with John Hohnsbeen (dead), who'd once been Peggy Guggenheim's curator, but Yiorgos was odious with him, maybe because he saw in him a dreaded, aged version of something he might become, an unemployed old man, a former beauty. John had a pale leather couch, and Yiorgos, after lotioning every part of his body, stretched out on it and ruined it. Instead of apologizing he reacted peevishly to John's excoriation. By this point I had no interest in sleeping with Yiorgos and he made it abundantly clear he had no interest in me, either. He complained of my snoring. Maybe that's why he'd lain on the couch: out of revenge.

The last few days we were together he'd been obsessed about whether he should join his friend Judy in Vienna or not. Every day he would draw me into debates as to whether he should pay to add on a flight to Vienna. The discussion gave me a massive headache. Just to have an opinion I argued against the extra expense. Privately I thought Vienna would be wasted on him, though he might find some promising queues of Americans to loiter in. What did he do in those lines? I knew it was August and he'd be obliged to wear shorts and a guinea T-shirt, which would treat his fellow citizens to a sight of his creamed muscles. Perhaps he could finagle his way into a discussion of his singing prospects. As you can see, I'm an equal opportunity hater.

* * *

I SAY I'VE SAID FAREWELL to S&M sex (maybe all sex) but I still respond to edgy personals. And if someone were to twist my nipples through my shirt, I would still fall in love. Getting ready to write this chapter, I wrote this poem that shows I'm still vulnerable despite my protestations:

The Interview (a poem)

Q. What was your best decade?
A. The 80s. I was in my 40s, still presentable,
living in Paris, learning French, becoming
known as a writer, HIV positive but in good
health, writing well.
Q. Best dick you've ever had?
A. I still haven't had yours yet.
Q. Your parents sound as if they were completely
crazy. How did you survive? By being gay?
A. Yes.
Q. How many more years will you live? You're
83 now.

A. Seven.

Q. Does death frighten you?

A. Terrifies me.

Q. What's the wisest thing you've learned?

A. Nothing, I guess.

Q. What's your best book?

A. I like them all.

Q. Who was the greatest love of your life?

A. Jim Ruddy in the sixties. I cried the most over him. That's what I do—cry over boys.

Q. Do you miss Paris?

A. No. Most of my friends there are dead.

Q. I have an apartment in Berlin. Why not spend a month there with me?

A. Okay.

Q. How excited does that make you? Percentagewise?

A. Fifty percent.

Q. Why the hesitation?

A. I'm afraid I'd fall in love with you. I've cried enough.

Sex with Straight Men

My college lover was so handsome—a sort of Paul Newman who walked around with his own pink baby spot on him—that two of the straight guys he worked with fell in love with him and put out (this was all before Stonewall, in 1969, made the barrier between straight and gay impermeable, and the advent of AIDS, in 1981, when the wall became impassable).

The other day I asked a gay twenty-seven-year-old champion athlete how you seduce straight guys (he's got several notches on his belt). He said, "You claim your college lover was handsome? No gay guy has looked at a man's face since 2020. No, you join a gym. You follow a sport and talk about it a lot, you chew tobacco ('packing lips,' we call it)—wear a jersey with some name on the back, keep saying 'sup,' act like everyone else (we call it 'blending') hive off with someone, then say to him, 'Dude, can I suck your dick?' "

"Subtle."

"Straight guys like to be sucked."

"Yeah. By girls."

"Wear some lipstick, then. My lover said to me that I might be a total bottom, but that there was nothing femme about me."

* * *

MY FIRST STRAIGHT WAS A guy at boarding school who told me he would be flunking out if he didn't write an English term paper for a heartless master, whom we called the Herm because his name was Herman Gottfried. I said I would dictate to him, that it would be easy since I'd already written my own essay on Dryden's *Hind and the Panther*, in which the snow-white hind is the Catholic Church, who tries to convince the panther (the Church of England) that he should obey the pope. There were several stanzas on transubstantiation, which seemed a curious subject for animals to debate.

Bobby was thrilled that I was going to help him. Midway through the *dictée*, I told him I wasn't going to finish unless he let me suck his dick. He was excited but angry, pulled his erection angrily out of his trousers. I sank to my knees and after the python had swallowed the lion cub continued with my seventeenth-century emblems. Funny thing—I had gotten an A-minus, and he got an A-plus, which proved improvisation was better than deliberation. He never said hi to me again.

My next straight was a glamorous blond quarterback named Bucky. When it wasn't football season, he had to take gym class with the rest of us nerds. I always sat on his feet while he was doing sit-ups and we'd switch. We both belonged to the butt club, a basement room where we could smoke for fifteen minutes after study hall and before lights out. It had posters on the wall, which would have been psychedelic ten years later but now were blurry bullfighting announcements. He seemed to like me, though I wasn't an athlete and my best friend wore Nazi regalia around the dormitory (later my friend became a tenderhearted socialist).

Bucky's father was a senator and they were rich. Though he played football his real forte was tennis and he had muscular legs covered with tiny gold hairs and white socks and the 1914 Arrow Shirt look, the straight nose and carved lips. You could just see him entering the room with his racket aloft or leaving with his pipe solemnly in his mouth. "Tennis, anyone?" Or he could be sailing with a girl with a headscarf. Years later when I got him on the phone, he seemed offended that I hadn't kept up with his career as a writer, but he wouldn't reveal what he'd published, if anything.

Every student had a one-man private room, probably to cut down on the English vice of buggery. Nor were we allowed out of our rooms after ten and lights out except to go to the toilet. I would often roost on one of the communal toilets to read on with my Rimbaud or Lautréamont. One night I snuck into Bucky's room. He was still awake. We had to whisper since suspicious masters would roam the corridors drunkenly, listening for miscreants to apprehend. Bucky acted as if it were perfectly normal that I'd decided to visit him after lights out. We whispered. I confided in him that there was a weird first-former (twelve years old) who liked to suck cock. He would visit me sometimes after lights out. Would Bucky be interested in a visit, too?

"Sure," he said. I could see he was getting an erection in his underpants.

"Well, it's me. I'm the cocksucker."

And he pulled down his Jockeys and released his hard dick with a thump on his hard stomach. I moved from a chair to his bed and touched his penis before it could run away. He put his hands behind his head and closed his eyes and concentrated and I engulfed his organ that wasn't too small or too big but just right—except my mouth was unsuitably dry from the daredevilry of my Big Bet that he'd be excited. I wasn't taught how to properly fellate until a real queen took me in hand in college, but I suppose the very act, like transubstantiation, was effective no matter in what hut or cave it was performed.

After he came, he stood next to the window, which seemed so poetic to me. Foucault said that courtship was the most romantic moment for heterosexuals but that for gays it was the aftermath, the taxi ride alone uptown. Looking at Bucky's slender, athletic body against the billowing white curtain was romantic distance enough for me.

Bucky asked me back, but I felt too guilty about "corrupting" him and said no. My sense of gay guilt was as great as my lust.

* * *

IN COLLEGE, ONCE IN THE height of my passion for a little straight wrestler, I threw myself into his arms weeping and declaring I knew my desire was sick, that I was in therapy to get well, but that a cure seemed still to be far off—and he got a hard-on and I went down on him, my face still wet with tears. Another kid, deliciously under washed, I accompanied in his truck into a cornfield, where he parked, turned off the headlights, stretched out, and lit up a joint. I'd been telling him that gays gave better blow jobs than girls and, with scientific curiosity, he pulled out a musty boner. When we'd finished, he said with ruthless objectivity, "That wasn't that much better." I'd forgotten that I was in a contest; I ignored the competition since I'd already had my tasty reward.

After I graduated, I moved to New York, where I met a young straight lawyer who became a good friend. He lived on Washington Square North, and I was always ringing his buzzer and having a drink or four with him and delivery pizza. He had ripe lips, bad skin, and smelled of testosterone. Once he stretched out on his couch, yawned, and pretended to be asleep—pure pretense since he had to raise his hips deliberately for me to slide his trousers down. We never spoke of it again; when I saw him years later, he was bald and proudly showed me photos of his lovely daughter. In my primitive way, I thought, I got some of that sperm that made her—a faggot's consolation, like a widow's mite, whatever that is.

Being a boss makes you a straight-cock magnet, a jock melter, or so I found out the year I lived in San Francisco and was an editor of a magazine. Just outside my office was the water fountain and I noticed that my most manly employee seemed unusually dehydrated. He visited the fountain ten times a day and each time, while leaning over the jet, stole a side glance at me. He was twenty-four, had been a star college football player, was clever, and was living with a beautiful blonde gymnast. I gathered that they were both interested in me, God knows why; I smoked four packs a day and drank a half bottle of Scotch and already had a ballooning waistline.

The young woman was *sans façon*, "unceremonious," not rude but direct, uncomplicated, whereas the guy had that straight male gaze of sizing up the competition, of computing your weak and strong points—just a shade of evaluation, nothing that interfered with his good manners or enthusiasm. Maybe an athlete's reserve can easily be interpreted as slightly judgmental, especially if the judged feels physically inferior.

We had many drinks together one night and they followed my car out across the Golden Gate Bridge to where I was living in the Berkeley Hills in an arts-and-crafts house a friend had lent me. There I sat apart from them and sipped a whiskey. They told me that my driving was dangerously alcoholic and it was a miracle I was still alive (they weren't preachy but caring). I really was drunk so I didn't get up to accompany them out to their car.

We finally had sex, all three of us, in New York after our magazine folded. In a friend's borrowed apartment. Again lots of drink. Sex consisted of the gymnast and me sucking her boyfriend's cock. Then I watched him fuck her. After that, on another occasion I had sex with him alone. He kissed and everything. But I never saw him again.

Another guy who worked with me was a hipster with an arcane vocabulary, lots of tattoos, and hair curling on his neck, someone who smoked as much as I did. He was another who visited the watercooler but stole more blatant glances into my office. He didn't so much walk as slouch and he had no butt, though he was young. Sitting on his fleshless bones must have been painful to him. Three times he said, "Knock, knock," and came into my office. He wanted to know once what my taste in music was; his was strictly heavy metal. Mine was Bach, Mahler, and Ravel. He invited me to go for a beer with him after work, and I did. We talked about our colleagues, the ones we liked and didn't like. I asked him to give me the backstory of his tattoos. The third time we talked books and favorite authors. His: Roald Dahl. Mine: Chekhov. I'd never read Dahl. Then we talked about a cover story we'd just run on Nabokov.

Back in New York he came by my cockroach-ridden third-floor walk-up studio with the bars on the window (I'd hired a former burglar to burglarproof my apartment after my meager belongings had been stolen, a loss I'd gaily greeted by declaring, "Oh, well, private property is theft, anyway"). It was the 1970s in New York and I was a sentimental socialist—an essential part of my identity as an "intellectual," a designation that poor but educated Americans such as me scoffed at but privately embraced.

My hipster, Craig, approved of my insouciance about theft. We both sat on my thin, stained couch and smoked a joint and giggled although nothing was funny except existence.

Once I got his jeans off him, I admired his baggy boxer shorts; I didn't know you could even wear them under tight jeans, but they looked authentically heterosexual to me, a little fuggy, which was all the better to my anthropological nose. It turned out his buttocks were not deflated but just trim and without curves. He had a wilderness of long pale brown pubic hair around his uncircumcised cock. (Oh, I thought, his parents must have been beatniks.) His penis was family-size and drooling. I went down on him in a trice. My mouth was dry from the marijuana.

And before you knew it, with all those "establishing" shots edited out by the "stupefier," as the French say (*le stupéfiant*), he had my knees around my ears and had plunged balls deep into my rectum. He was riddling me ecstatically and bruising my mouth with cigarette-heavy lips and even biting me when suddenly he reared back in a sudden horror of awareness (a man!), pulled out of me, wriggled into his jeans with his dirty brown cock, and stepped into his sneakers, leaving his black-soled tube socks behind, and was out the door and thumping his way all three flights down to the street and, I assume, running and running. I felt shocked/pleased that I'd been able to frighten him so deeply. I never heard from him again.

Fuck Buddies

IN THE 1970S FOLLOWING STONEWALL and before AIDS, no one gay was afraid of promiscuity. Typically one had a lover with whom one shared an apartment and a leather handcraft store in the Village; though the marriage was sexless, one had tricks (one-night stands) and a circle of fuck buddies, regulars who dropped by for a casual fuck. We thought we'd broken marriage and opened it up to the consanguinity and fun of tribal love. We were no longer two atoms but long chains of molecules. Our marriages were open; we loved different people for a whole host of reasons, not one at a time but all together.

Not that my fuck buddies got together many times—maybe only four or five times. One of our lovers was a big American Indian who wasn't completely sane (he had a conspiracy theory that a group of older men were plotting to sacrifice him to the sun god). He believed that every second of his life was being filmed and, as in a Philip K. Dick sci-fi novel, everyone was in on the game. He'd look at us with real fear from time to time and a disabused smile on his face, as if he could see through our hypocritical affection. He knew better. He knew we were secretly sharpening our knives for our ritual slaughter.

He was never quite on the same wavelength as the rest of us, but he was generous with his amazing body—his broad chest, his big cock, his fleshy arms, his plush legs. He wasn't thin or fat but fleshy and brown as a well-fed partridge at the start of hunting season, not taut like a gay gym rat but silky, warm to the touch, masculine, inviting, the way your father's body felt to you as a child when you were awakened by a nightmare and got into his bed. That was the contradiction—psychologically he was a jangled mess but physically he emanated calm. Eventually he pushed his mother down the stairs and was confined to an institution for the criminally insane, the worst kind of sentence since it's left up to a judge to determine when the prisoner is "ready" to be released. In bed, before madness had overwhelmed him, he was kind if puzzled, happy to top us all but unsure of our intentions.

My occasional roommate, the Norwegian flight attendant, was another sweetheart, but in his case he had no brooding dark side. He liked and admired everyone. And everyone liked him. When I first met him, he *was* echt

Minnesota—pure, friendly, guileless. But after several years in New York, he became wry and sophisticated, a little satirical gleam lit up his eye, though he remained just as sweet. I've often to my shame spoken in superlatives; he couldn't help teasing me about my exaggerations, but since he's the very person the quaint Americanism *down-to-earth* was invented for, he was always kind. Never again would he be Midwestern bland once he had that edgy twinkle in his eye, which the French call *malicieux*, meaning "sly," not "malicious."

We'd lie around with the sexy Indian and the comely Norwegian and whoever else had dropped by on, say, a Thursday afternoon, and before long we'd be stoned and kissing one another and feasting on hard cock. It was a golden moment in life—my life, certainly, but maybe in modern history. To be carefree, young, loving, promiscuous, and post religious, free of grim American "morality"—it was only a parenthetical decade between much darker periods. Maybe we were a bit childlike then—natural, uncolonized. The widespread use of drugs, and later the advent of AIDS, made life more driven (not for me—I was never a serious druggie) and eventually tragic. AIDS made us fear sex, though, in a Russian roulette way, we still pursued it. We would never again enjoy sex in a happy, unworried arcadian way. By the time the curse of AIDS had been lifted, age and experience had spoiled our simple delight. Age doesn't make us wiser but provides us with more grudges. When we're young, our personality is less formed and we fit, tongue and groove, with more people, many people, anyone who likes us; the years, however, add more features, only some of them pleasant, and with our sharp edges we can tolerate few friends—and fewer fuck buddies.

Rory

I HAVE A YOUNG HALF-FILIPINO friend named Rory, an ex-student, a star athlete, an award-winning poet, and someone who has become a sexless lover, though he is half a century younger than me. Not that he doesn't want to have sex with ancient, obese old me. We share a bed when he's in town. He once woke me up with his hard dick in my sleeping hand and asked me to jerk him off. I did, just to be nice, but the next time I told him to leave me alone.

I was flattered of course. Being an old libertine, I had no moral scruples, but I had been impotent for a year and didn't want to fake desire. And my pagan worship of beauty wouldn't let me touch his perfect body with my liver-spotted hands. He reminded me that in Kawabata's *House of the Sleeping Beauties* the old men, ashamed of their bodies, slept with prostitutes who were drugged asleep—all fine until one country girl died of an overdose, leading the madam to point out there were more where she came from. García Márquez was so taken by the plot that he copied it in his last, controversial novel *Memories of My Melancholy Whores*, banned in Iran.

As it turned out, Rory, who lived in San Francisco, became my Scheherazade. Almost every night he would Skype me and tell me about his latest erotic adventure. I'm sure many of my American readers, if they've come this far, are groaning about how I could "exploit" this youth and complaining about how perverted this sounds. What more do they expect of a pervert? In fact our age difference (he was thirty) didn't register with him; he called me "twin" since our rotten values were the same, our experiences, our likes and dislikes. I think I was a mild force for good since I convinced him to go for a PhD in Japanese (a language he could already speak but not read since he'd worked in Uniqlo for a year in Tokyo).

Rory had a horrible incestuous mother and mine was flirtatious when drunk every night, so like good Americans we could complain of our man-eating moms until that bored us. He was a Japanese fashion plate and was always showing me his new black kimono or T-shirt sporting a manga monster or the chic wool skirt he'd inherited from his grandmother or my vintage Yamamoto jacket I'd outgrown. His upwardly mobile parents had urged him into becoming a squash champion, the sport of CEOs. He got a thrill out of slamming into defeat the tall lean white straight boys he was in love with, guys who would enrage him when they wouldn't let him blow them.

★ ★ ★

You're a proud bottom (except when you get off by being humiliated) but unlike most fuckees, you're fierce, combative, anything but a ladyboy. In one of your poems, you say a teacher said no one could identify your type (we write nightly poems to each other that link up with words the other one used the day before, our poor-man *renga*, as the Japanese call their competitive group poem cycles).

In fact we love everything traditionally Japanese—Kyoto's sand-and-stone gardens, the samurai's love of boys (I just sent you a copy of the seventeenth-century *The Great Mirror of Male Love*), Kawabata's novels *Snow Country* and *The Sound of the Mountain*, the seventeenth-century *Essays in Idleness*, in which we learn that frayed silk is more beautiful than new silk, that a house shouldn't be too orderly. Now I'm reading *Tales of Idolized Boys: Male-Male Love in Medieval Japanese Buddhist Narratives.* Tanizaki wrote in his *In Praise of Shadows* that Japanese bathrooms with their wooden seats and pine boughs for plumbing were superior to Western surgically gleaming toilets, just as the "muddy" complexion of Japanese people was more appealing than the white faces of Europeans. The broken and mended tea-ceremony cup would sell for tens of thousands of dollars if it had an ancient Korean pedigree, passed down from famous tea masters, much more prized than a new perfect cup.

Rory understood this esthetic, if he seldom practiced it. He wanted to be a winner; no *Nobility of Failure* for him. If he couldn't seduce a new slim white boy every night, he went into a depression and I'd have to cajole him out of the abyss. If a professor seemed reluctant to write him a recommendation, he'd hit bottom, though the professor might relent the next day. Rory would be riding high if three or four white men were sending him messages in a day, but would do fifty more squats if they all went dark. He was always reviewing them, like a gambler evaluating his cards. Tonight would it be the King of Hearts (the well-spoken man who became tender after a sadistic fuck) or the Ace of Clubs (the guilt-ridden sixty-year-old married man from Michigan)?

Rory sometimes wondered how had preppy white become his *main taste*? His best childhood friend was Black, someone who had encouraged him to be fearless, a boundary-breaking straight guy with good manners and a hilarious sense of humor who came to dinner one night. Rory imitated Black ghetto speech, listened to hip-hop on his big headphones, proudly showed me a snapshot of him with five young straight Black dudes who took him in as a "person of color." But his ideal was a hung skinny white man, someone who was an awkward dancer, and generally clueless. One night on Skype, Rory and I started constructing White Man. He had an Irish setter, this was his third time at Burning Man, he loved his mom, his dad would get drunk in his den, listen to Johnny Mathis and cry. At deb parties White Man would slow dance with grandmothers just to be polite. He pretended to like fly-fishing with his dad but, in reality, it bored him. On Sundays as a boy he'd wear a white surplicer and carry the Cross, which went well with his blond hair. As a teen, he wasn't out with anyone except his best friend, Amelia, a Chinese gal pal. They would swoon in secret over Steve, the head prefect of their tony coed boarding school, St. Eustache.

Predictable, even risible, as White Man is, Rory finds him irresistible. Theoretically Rory would prefer Black people or other Asians, but white cock is the only thing that turns him on. He likes circumcised men because they're more American. He prefers pubic hair that hasn't been gardened but is wild and overgrown. He can spend hours daydreaming about cocks drooling precum, doubling in size when fully erect, smelling of sweat and hormones—as though his ideal joins an angelic head, blond and fine featured, to an almost gruesomely bestial penis—Ariel and Caliban in one person. And don't let him get onto the nearly holy mysteries of unwiped male bottoms . . .

I remember once inviting Gore Vidal to dinner and promising him cute boys and he nearly shouted, "That's the last thing I want." At my vast age I sympathize with this aversion, at least "in person," but Rory is my last connection to a reality-fantasy that has obsessed me for sixty-five years. He's my only tenuous grasp on the life force, on Eros.

Whenever we Skype, he's walking briskly through Oakland, which is dangerous. In my shrinking violet way, I'm always worrying he'll be besieged by a teen gang wanting his expensive high-tops or his manga shirts. He could be vexed by my urge to protect him, but he takes it the right way. He knows I care for him. I suppose I've seen him once or twice at rest but mostly he's in motion. "You have to remember I'm manic," he says. It's true he takes six pills a day, including lithium. He's often claiming he's crazy, and when he gets blackout drunk, he does act like a madman. White Man finds him all the more fascinating, of course. He says one of his pills makes him sleep too much, but when he changed it recently to something less soporific, he felt as if his head were on fire, that all his medications had permanently damaged his brain. "Temporarily," I concede, knowing nothing about it.

He wants to be a great writer, which I'm afraid is a matter less of talent and more of persistence, finding a niche, enduring rejection. Or as Proust put it, you must be stupid to write, if that means not being too clever, too experimental. Once the very seasoned composer Virgil Thomson said to me, when he was seventy-four and I thirty, that inventing things out of thin air was suitable for the short run but that imitation of life was the only way to make art over a long life (a curious observation for a composer). I think he's right. Oh, and it helps to have a verbal knack, a silver tongue, but it's not necessary. Willa Cather had it; Theodore Dreiser did not, but he's almost as good as she.

Rory knows that he's beautiful and often says he's determined to enjoy this part of his life—young, not so dumb, and full of cum. White Man is impressed by his poetry, athleticism, riotous good moods, lust.

He's also periodically insecure. Three guys can be after him but if the fourth neglects him, he goes into a tailspin. More squats. He likes children and they like him, partly because he's so cool—and such a kid. He teaches fourth grade and over the summer he's coaching squash with what he calls the "brown kids." Sometimes he Skypes me right after a game and it's fun to see his hair, normally straight as grass, ringleted with sweat and his tan face white with exhaustion.

He never criticizes my writing, only gives me encouragement, which Gertrude Stein said is all a writer ever needs. Once I was walking bent over and Rory told me to "tighten my core"—the only advice he's ever given me. Twice I've told him not to get blackout drunk. I've learned that advice is pointless, but I couldn't resist giving it those two times.

Here's one of the *renga* poems I wrote him (my word was *breathe*). He sent me a photo of his naked body from the back, standing in a window against a dawn sky:

I couldn't breathe for an instant
When I saw you standing naked
Looking out in the high open window,
An immense slab of flawless sky
After a sleepless night of near sex
Both of you wanting to be screwed
But loving in your frustration, Warm
Brothers as the German say, a heat
That left you as golden as the fleetest
Deity, except I couldn't see the wings on your
heels.

Jean Genet referred to a young lover as his "frail ambassador" to the world. Rory is slender but not frail; he's not my lover but he is my ambassador to life. He's always teaching me street talk. Did you know that "putting the brain on your man" is a whore's way of referring to sucking dick? I just learned that from Rory.

Sex and Literature

I'VE BEEN WRITING HOT FICTION since puberty so for me sex and literature have always been intertwined. I wrote about gay sex before I'd come out to friends and family, as though I needed to pen my identity before I pinned it down (as the son of Texans it was inevitable for me to make an *i* for *e* substitution—I pronounced *pen* as *pin*). It's as though I needed to imagine being gay before doing anything about it. My first unpublished novel, called either "Dark Currents" or "The Tower Window," written at boarding school when I was fourteen during evening study hall, invented the convenient alibi that one turned to boys after being rejected by a girl. Also, I discovered that I lost control of my narrative once I entered the thoughts of the teen hero, named significantly

Peter Cross, so I devised the method of deducing his thoughts uniquely from his facial expressions, a sort of psychic phrenology. Very clumsy but at least my method didn't drown me in streams of consciousness.

Over the years in my unpublished MSS I attributed my psycho form of horniness to my mother ("Mrs. Morrigan") or devised a love story between twin boys separated at birth, one rich the other poor ("The Amorous History of Our Youth"). Or I wrote about straight and gay friends perfectly accepting of one another and all in psychoanalysis. I forget the title of that one. I wrote a novel about the agonies of a middle-class white boy coming out (that one I called "The Beautiful Room Is Empty," a title I liked so much I recycled it for a later, published novel).

Then I won a prize for a play in college in which I tackled the themes of both homosexuality and race relations. It was called *The Blueboy in Black* and was staged starring Cicely Tyson in New York for a month. It was a flop but it triggered in me a decade of writing bad plays, in which I explored shifting genders (*Trios*), a Jewish lady given the first name Madame by her aspirational parents, a family condemned to repeat a murderous ritual—even a musical for which I got the rights to *Stage Door*, a 1936 comedy about a Broadway boardinghouse full of young actresses, written by Edna Ferber and George Kaufman. The composer of that one, a hopped-up little queen, hated my "book," probably for good reason, and abandoned the project.

* * *

FICTION HAS ALWAYS HAD THE reputation of being naughty. In the eighteenth and nineteenth centuries, it frequently was dirty, especially in France (and I'm not talking about pornography). I mean things like *Le Sopha* by Crébillon le Gai. Defoe's *Moll Flanders* records haphazardly her many marriages (some unwittingly incestuous), her life as a thief, the existence of her many children (most abandoned), a chance inheritance, her repentance, and a happy ending. A novel written in the time of Nero, the *Satyricon* by Petronius, has several horny female characters but the star is a teenage slave who is buggered by several men. *An Ephesian Tale*, written in the second century A.D. by Xenophon (not *that* Xenophon), follows a tedious teenage couple (straight) through all their Candide-like travails until at last, virginity miraculously intact, they are reunited. A parallel gay couple, after all their own misadventures, join them in a double wedding. Of course, Greek and Latin pastoral and funerary poetry is full of boy love, as are some of Shakespeare's sonnets and Marlowe's plays and most of sixteenth-century Turkish love poetry (if you were actually in love with a girl, decorum demanded you address her as a boy). Japanese Buddhist priests loved their *chigo* or acolytes and there are lots of sixteenth-century tales about them.)

In the twentieth century gay content became widespread—especially in France: Marcel Proust, Jean Genet, André Gide, Jean Cocteau, Marcel Jouhandeau, François Mauriac, and dozens of others. Eekhoud in Belgium, Kuzmin in Russia. Christopher Isherwood was the best and most open of the twentieth-century English gay writers, followed by Alan Hollinghurst. In the pre-Stonewall era James Baldwin was the best uncloseted American novelist. Now it seems to me all the most talented new novelists are gay—the Nigerian Arinze Ifeakandu; the Brits Thomas Grattan and Tom Crewe; in France, Édouard Louis; in Finland, Pajtim Statovci; in America, Garth Greenwell and Bryan Washington. I've met most of them; there's even an Edmund White award for the best new gay fiction.

I've been publishing gay fiction since the 1970s and would have brought out queer fiction in the 1960s if any editor had been brave enough to take me on (so many were closeted, too—with good reason, since coming out meant losing your job). My first published gayish novel was *Forgetting Elena* (1973), which seems to be about the rituals of gay men on Fire Island but also seems to be about court culture in medieval Japan. The protagonist is an amnesiac who is ashamed of his lapsed memory and accordingly models his behavior and talk on other people's expectations. He has even forgotten what (heterosexual) sex is and experiences it as painful as it is pleasurable or a code that may function bizarrely as a way of signifying nonverbal messages. The local houses are full of males, organized hierarchically. The book was itself indirect in its representations of homosexual life.

My next novel, *Nocturnes for the King of Naples* (1978), was still experimental but much more openly gay. It is a letter addressed to a dead lover (who may be me or God!). It draws on the long tradition, going back to Rumi and St. John of the Cross, of confusing sex and piety, the deity with the beloved, an expression that reaches its acme in the baroque (think of Bernini's sculpture the *Ecstasy of St. Teresa*, in which St. Michael stabs the writhing body of the lady saint). The hushed opening scene occurs in some version of the ruined cruising pier at the foot of Christopher Street, described almost as though it were a cathedral. There are scarcely detectable poems (couplets, a sonnet, a sestina) seeded here and there written out as prose.

After these experimental books I turned to autobiographical fiction, transparently realistic because by this point I'd decided to record my own homosexual life, a subject already difficult for the average reader to understand and therefore one that should be treated straightforwardly. Eventually, to my surprise, the enterprise became a trilogy: *A Boy's Own Story* (1982), *The Beautiful Room Is Empty* (1988), and *The Farewell Symphony* (1997). *A Boy's Own Story* I wrote about male-male teenage sex;

in *Beautiful Room* I turned cottaging into a wedding and ended with the Stonewall uprising exploring my gay subject from many angles, I wrote *Caracole* about straight fops, and *Jack Holmes and His Friend* about a passionate friendship between a gay man and a straight man that doesn't end up in bed. *The Married Man*, an AIDS story about a bisexual man, became a Franco-American love story in which one of the participants is a liar. In *The Farewell Symphony*, the last volume of the trilogy, withholding sex as a punishment is one of the themes. Sex = death is another. My best novel, *Hotel de Dream* (2007), takes place in the 1890s and the protagonist is Stephen Crane, the straight author of *The Red Badge of Courage*. He wrote a novel about a girl prostitute, *Maggie: A Girl of the Streets*, and intended to publish one about a boy prostitute, then he died at age twenty-eight. I tried to tell his story, his marriage to Cora, the madam of a Florida house of prostitution called Hotel de Dream, the story of the boy, and the fate of Crane's novel about him. Recent novels of mine—*A Saint from Texas*, *A Previous Life*, and *The Humble Lover*—have dealt with polyamory and bisexuality and intergenerational polarities, which have become fashionable subjects because now AIDS, if treated, is no longer fatal in the first world.

I've always argued that my frequent, explicit sex scenes—straight, gay, and lesbian—have never been pornographic. Pornography, as Susan Sontag pointed out, is a sex aid and therefore should not contain distractions or longueurs but should use basic Anglo-Saxon words and stick to the rhythm of one-handed reading. Most writers in English today have decided it's impossible to write about sex without falling into cliché, but that decision seems to relate only to pornography. Real erotic writing, as Colette or Kawabata, for instance, have shown, is sensual without being sentimental, unpredictable, startling, an odd mixture of femininity and masculinity, the spiritual and the human, and frequently funny, especially when the body fails the imagination. I've never understood why sex should be excluded from serious fiction, since it is a language one speaks and one's partner never understands, which is both communal and isolating.

Humor in the form of self-satire or in the examination of cultural differences has always marked my fiction, which is both sociological and psychological. Sociological because I think class and regional origins play a determining role in shaping character—but sociology almost always takes a back seat to psychology, since in a democracy such as the United States people can change accents, manners, schools, jobs, regions. and escape their background.

Does sex play reveal character? It can reveal repressed desires. I knew a Texas tycoon who was never allowed to top anyone because he was so little. When he finally met a compliant bottom, he married him in an elaborate ceremony years before gays could marry legally. I knew two bottoms who fell in love, passive partly because they were both insecure and it's less risky to throw your legs over your head ("heels over head in love," we used to say) than to take charge, penetrate, and keep it up. But these bottoms, once they became more confident through their relationship, turned into two tops and sought out a third person they could sodomize (for a while I was lucky Pierre). I knew a beautiful Swede who was so boring in bed I'd watch TV while he fucked me, in contrast to a sweet Georgia peach who would shudder and shout when he climaxed. Was he secretly an ecstatic? Perhaps. He was certainly an avowed neurotic mess who would declare his undying love one day and then vanish for a month or two. An Italian stud who broke my heart (the hero of my novel *A Previous Life*) could cum only after hours of throttling his dick in prolonged infanticide, but he would explain away his coitus reservatus as a form of "edging." He would also tremble and shake when he finally did cum, an hour later.

I usually try to get sex out of my love affairs early on by pursuing other bottoms (who as I've mentioned are usually the nicer people) or by growing cold after a month of delirium. Hell if I know why I do that. My Italian stallion, despite his tedious "edging," always kept sex in our relationship until we ended it altogether. But only his lordly persistence (which I admired) kept sex in our bedroom for three years. I am oddly lesbian in my taste for sexlessness, for slippered tea and friendship, for "Boston" marriage, after a short season of lust.

For me, sex is better on the page. Maybe I find it less menacing, more exciting in literature rather than in the bedroom. Everyone is free to have his or her Freudian speculation about my oddities. Maybe sex is so important to me that it shouldn't exist as an uncontrolled experiment. Maybe I'm so susceptible to its blandishments that it must be limited, like a nuclear experiment, to a small, remote island of the psyche. Maybe my pre-Stonewall youthful formation left me with such abiding guilt feelings that the cost-benefit ratio of pleasure to shame is narrow.

Of course the real anguish of passion lies in being rejected. Normally the fear of rejection, even if it's unheralded and unprovoked, is just as bad as the real thing. Passion is an uneasy bedfellow. Iris Murdoch, the great English novelist, writes of "the splendor and violence of love." And says of unrequited passion, "That love can be so strong and so entirely powerless is what breaks the heart." Splendid and violent, strong and powerless—that's the truth of a passion that's not returned or that one fears won't last.

Not that sex and passion are identical. The passionate (male) lover is so awed by the beloved that he is sometimes impotent, as in *Armance* by Stendhal. I remember a moment in Max Ophül's film *La Ronde* in which a young man lies disconsolate beside his older female lover. He has obviously just had a fiasco and says something like "I've heard young men are impotent the first three or four times," and she says dryly, "I think it's the first one or two times," and exhales her cigarette smoke.

Am I alone in thinking the passionate lover is so jealous he doesn't mind if the beloved doesn't put out as long as she or he doesn't sleep with anyone else, that he would gladly adopt chastity if it guaranteed fidelity?

Am I the only one who believes hopeless love serves to upend a too well-ordered life so that it can flourish, that love is a way of moving a plant from a small box that it's outgrown into a larger one to give it a new, more flourishing life, though transplanting, if it doesn't work, might risk the organism's very existence?

Why do novelists write so much about love? To beat Pan's drum and play his fife? Is it to introduce the irrational into the pattern, the way abstract expressionists, when their canvas had become too "tight," would invite another painter to come in and "ruin" the composition so that the original artist could see new possibilities, have to resolve random, unforeseen tensions?

Or is passionate love, like paranoia, a way of tying all the disparate events together? Of plugging wires into new, improbable sockets on the switchboard? Or, of simply ending the book? As Nabokov said, an epistolary novel begins in the post office and ends in the church. Now we could say it ends in the psych ward.

Love is something almost all of us can identify with. Strange loves are still a variation on a familiar model, though the gay love of the recent past—unbridled and sequential and hyper-horny—might have been too Martian for most people to sympathize with unless it was tragic. There's no fag like a dead fag. What was that joke? Hi, Mom, first the bad news. I'm gay. Then the good—I have AIDS and I'm dying. Lesbian couples can be forgiven by society for existing and not shaving under their arms if they move to the country, and many of them do in fact rusticate. Gay men are okay if they do your hair and listen to your outraged stories about that heel, your hubby—or if they play the grand piano and keep their morbid sexuality out of sight. Proust got away with describing even gay sadism and gerontophilia by deriving general (preferably botanical) principles from them.

Nabokov was able to resuscitate the romantic novel by making it about pedophilia. Maybe a great contemporary novelist could write about Romeo and Romeo if they married, adopted, and joined the PTA or preferably died. In the past gay writers adopted Proust's Albertine strategy, pretending Albert was Albertine, which sometimes made them great observers of women to render the substitution credible. At the very least it made them good liars with good memories. Isn't fiction called "lies like truth?"

Everyone is so constrained in his or her identity that straights are reluctant to write about gays. Maybe they're afraid their friends will suspect *they* are gay. Or that gays will berate them for trespassing or for lack of knowledge or compassion. Gays of course are allowed to write about straights, although in the 1960s one critic made a fuss that in *Who's Afraid of Viginia Woolf?* Edward Albee was maligning straight marriage by basing it on real-life neurotic gay misalliances. Tennessee Williams was often found guilty of similarly unsavory gay-straight transpositions. In the same period straight novelists tackled gay subjects. I've argued that the most brilliant gay comic novel is *Pale Fire* by that inveterate heterosexual Nabokov. And Iris Murdoch's *A Fairly Honourable Defeat*, written in 1970 by a married Oxford don just three years after homosexuality was legalized in Britain, is the most three-dimensional portrait of a gay marriage, according to Garth Greenwell.

The Horrors of Adolescence

My sister and I were raised in such a damaging, incestuous family that it's a miracle that we did not grow up to be axe murderers. Our mother always told us to count our blessings, and unlike a third of the world's children who go to bed hungry every night, we were well nourished and clothed. We lived in a heated house, our tuition was paid, our linen was washed, and we were given some of the advantages (piano lessons for me, summer camp for my sister). Although we were nominally Christian Scientist, we saw doctors when we were sick. Of course middle-class American children don't compare themselves to those in misery in the developing world, but to members of their own "reference group."

My sister, after being impregnated as a thirteen-year-old by our father and having a miscarriage and several suicide attempts, became a happy, productive, feeling therapist, the mother of three biological children and of eight adopted children, two of them HIV positive. Now in her eighties she is as dynamic and hardworking as ever. She's writing her own memoir and I don't want to steal her thunder.

My mother colonized every corner of my mind she could understand and made me pick her blackheads and put her into her Merry Widow foundation garment. She was a psychologist for brain-damaged and intellectually disabled children. In the car on long trips, I would read to her from the sacred writings of Bruno Bettelheim, who had invented the now thoroughly rejected theory of autism being caused by the "refrigerator mother." In his own Chicago clinic, the Orthogenic School, he would beat his patients in public and in some cases assure them they would never marry or get a job. This man we revered turned out to be a sadistic fake, nearly as fraudulent as mother's other thought impresario, Mary Baker Eddy.

A Harvard psychologist, Steven Pinker, reports in *The Blank Slate* on a study of identical twins raised together whose lives turned out very differently; one became homosexual, for instance, and one did not, which suggests neither nature nor nurture is determinative. That something like "character" might ultimately shape behavior. Without bragging, I wonder which elements in my own past led me to become a professor at Princeton and the author of thirty-two books instead of a wastrel and drunk—because I still believe in determining forces, though I concede they can scarcely be measured. Oh, and I was a drunk for twenty years.

My mother was convinced most of the time that I was a "genius" and wrote her master's thesis on the gifted child and (I think) religion. This conviction on her part was wavering ("How do we really know you're so bright?" she would sometimes ask. "It hasn't been proven"). At other times she would imagine I was "spiritual" and "sensitive" and have me read the life of Nijinsky, the schizophrenic homosexual dancer, just as a hint as to the price talent must pay. Sometimes she would tell me with tears in her eyes that if I weren't her son, she would marry me ("I wish I could meet a man like you," she'd say when I was ten). She would indulge my whims. When I decided I was a Buddhist, she traveled thirty miles to the South-side Buddhist Church and took me afterward to a shabby sukiyaki lunch at a Japanese restaurant where the proprietors had recently gone through a difficult war. If I wanted to study the harp, she'd pay for lessons. I was told that my grade school teachers worried because I displayed an unusual degree of empathy toward adults for a child (perhaps they couldn't bring themselves to say I was a fawning little prat).

I don't want to make my mother sound like a monster. She did, usually, believe in me, though her notion of a genius was of total instant mastery of any subject to which one turned one's attention, which made brilliance during the first harp lesson discouragingly remote, stood in my way of learning quadratics and physics and even driving. I was "good" at improvising tone poems to a brook on the piano until my father couldn't bear my banging any longer and held his hands over his ears. Doesn't an irritated parent say to his little prodigy, "I think we've been amused quite enough tonight?" I was "good" at poetry and doggedly wrote hundreds of unmetered rhymed couplets to all four of the seasons. I was "good" at writing a biography of Peter the Great, but gave it up after a couple of days copying the standard work. I based a third grade play on one by Molnár; my mother rented a king's costume for me. My fourth grade play was *The Death of Hector,* based on the *Iliad*; I played Hector and the cutest boy in school played Achilles and killed me. At summer camp I wore a red Hudson Bay blanket and played Boris Godunov staggering around in my mad scene with the Mussorgsky opera pounding from the speakers. In seventh grade my tea boxes paraded past my music boxes in a royal ceremony.

In my forties I had a group therapist who arranged for me to be the king, all the other group members bowed—and then, nothing. I hadn't ever got beyond my arrival in my monarchical fantasies. *Forgetting Elena* also ended with the prince's big arrival, followed by . . . nothing! For me being a king or a god was just a matter of arriving and being acknowledged; I was as bad as the Republicans at governing. I just wanted to be elected.

I guess I picked up from my mother that one should always reach out for help. When I was seven and my parents divorced and we moved out of our house to a hotel in a pretty Cincinnati suburb, I roamed the streets by myself, found a Presbyterian minister in his office, and told him of our family woes. I locked myself in the bathroom sobbing, "I did it! I did it!" until the staff removed the locked door and fished me out. I didn't just quietly cut myself or kill myself; I made a scene until even my alcoholic mother noticed.

Maybe homosexuality saved me, or else being a heavily disguised criminal child did the trick. My father would put us children in a day care center and then forget to pick us up in the evening. In revenge I would take a couple of the cigarettes he put out in small silver vases for guests and smoke them in the basement toilet at the day care center. Later, when I figured out what homosexuality was (my mother briefed me on a gay camper who was "acting out" at Camp Whispering Pines and told me not to get alone with him), I cornered him and sucked my very first sticky, throbbing red penis—before denouncing him to the counselors, just as at my boarding school I sucked off our stoned jazz instructor and denounced him, not for homosexuality but for getting the boys high on marijuana. He was fired right away. I sent a love letter to a gym teacher, a French Canadian champion runner, but he (wisely) didn't respond. I sent another letter to a bald homosexual painter who taught at the neighboring art academy, but he merely reproached me the next time I saw him. I wept, I contemplated suicide, I read the sutras. I begged my father to send me to a therapist and he finally agreed. The shrink was totally mad and had us hack with axes at stumps in the backyard labeled MOM and DAD. I saw him for four years until he was hauled off raving to the Karl Menninger clinic in Topeka, Kansas.

For me being gay was a way of giving the world homeopathic doses of my inner rage; betrayal was my normal mode of treating my partners, including Bob Hamilton, my mother's fiancé's dishy son. I was a seemingly mild boy full of inner rage. I didn't show my hand. No one except my "victims" at boarding school knew I was gay, though a few suspected. I would talk a good game about how to excite women, how to stimulate the clitoris into multiple orgasms, but it was all just talk gleaned from the few books about sex I could find. Mostly I relied on the braggadocio of older, more experienced boys; their exploits I repeated as my own.

For me the most thrilling part of the day was the communal shower after gym class. The sight of boys' naked bodies—not the penis size, not the amount of pubic hair, not the muscles in the legs, arms, chest—none of these details did I fetishize, but just the sight of so much nakedness in motion made me weak. Of course I knew that close as these males were, they couldn't be touched or even studied for long. My hungry eyes must not linger but keep moving in feigned indifference. I loved the smooth white buttocks under a pink glaze of hot water, the water drops constituting the St. Catherine's lace in an armpit, that web of tiny pale blossoms, the pink cheeks under a dark, uncurled skullcap of wet hair, the crystalline runoff from a dangling finger, like God's reaching to touch Adam's, the burnished columnar nape turning above the jittery play of shoulder muscles reflecting and shattering the bright overhead light. One guy had a big, ropy dick, like an upside-down caduceus, where the snakes were veins, the wings were balls. I loved the smell of cheap soap, the laundered reek of towels wrapping small adolescent waists, outfitted with more subtle but pronounced muscles than any adult's . . .

Readers complained that the adolescent hero of my most popular novel, *A Boy's Own Story*, behaved so badly, betraying his adult sex partner, but I argued that how could the product of an oppressive culture not be deformed? I didn't go crazy, though my mother, who as a psychologist was constantly testing us, said my Rorschach results were troubling since I saw in the inkblots only diamonds and graveyards. I met a sexy farmer on the train and decided to write an opera about him called *Orville*. I didn't get beyond the first half of the overture. I decided to paint scary self-portraits that looked like Fayum mummy pictures. I tried to seduce my best male friend, who didn't see me for two years afterward. I did skate over pretty thin ice. My mother sent me at age thirteen to the best Freudian in Evanston, Illinois. I had just been reading *The Picture of Dorian Gray* and couldn't keep myself from constant campy quipping. The Freudian told my mother I should be institutionalized and the key thrown away, a diagnosis she immediately repeated to me.

Did art save my life? Or sucking cock? Has it been saved? How can an atheist be saved?

I sometimes think of my kind of autobiographical writing as spider's work, as pulling big glistening webs out of one's very body, of searching about for the twigs to attach one's floating gossamer constructions to, as bodying forth sticky patterned threads, the silk extruded by one's spinnerets, meant to catch something—maybe just a creature's attention or its nourishing substance. When the writer-spider has spun all his silk, must he stop secreting?

When I was a dangerously unbalanced teen, I used to think that I could program all the ink flowing out of me by reading crucial books or watching influential films or programming certain classical music, as if I weren't admittedly subject to suggestions, but my job was to choose them.

Sex acts—which gave me a sinking, inevitable feeling, the sense of a catastrophe—were exciting, damaging invasions into my equanimity, the rotten-orange smell of ether, mammoth, unforgettable, ridden with guilt, like a tarnished mirror that has lost its silvery backing and shows the face only in diseased splotches. For me sucking someone was momentous, a clear sign that I was "sick," irretrievable. Only by writing about these dark events (remember my first unpublished manuscript, a gay novel, was called "Dark Currents") could I turn them into gold. I wrote to keep my head above water. I was drowning in my own weirdness, my exclusion from the human race, my hermaphroditic nature.

But I knew that what I was writing would never be read.

GIOVANNI

What's left of an ex in my memory?
He was kind and courtly (as he should have been
Since he was a Sicilian aristocrat),
When he wasn't being horrid if I stepped
Out of line, then frozen with fury and
Unforgiving. He taught me one good pasta
Recipe, Pasta alla Norma, with fried eggplant. He
Bought me a CD player when mine broke, several
Cashmere blankets and he restored a leather
Club chair that was in tatters. He was a doctor,
  could play
The harpsichord, cook a few dishes, entertain
In his battleship-sized loft, lie and cheat
  convincingly,
Make the sort of love a heterosexual
  Mediterranean
Male might make, selfish and athletic—and which
  I liked
Because it never dwindled away even after we
  broke up.
We both cried a lot. He had a black Ceramic vase
  with an

African face and a crown, until I explained that
Was unacceptable in politically correct New York.
Then it was banished, as was I when I told his new
Lover that Giovanni and I were still having sex.
  I saw a good shrink
And got over him. I'll never have another lover—
Too much of a bother. Once in a while I wish we
  could
Speak on the phone, to find out whether his father's
Parkinson's is progressing, whether his little brother
Got married, and did he ever discover a cure for that
Kind of breast cancer. And does he still hate me?

ACKNOWLEDGMENTS

I never had such a brilliant editor as Daniel Loedel, who urged me on to greater coherence, passion, and self-revelation. I know I failed to deliver, that I often "wandered," like the old man I am spinning random anecdotes after dinner over brandy, that I didn't want to repeat the erotic adventures recounted in earlier books, that my fatal attraction to self-satire often robbed my pages of the seriousness one owes to a summing up, but whatever value and sequential sense *The Loves of My Life* possesses is due to the thousand notes Daniel gave me. In American publishing it's a cliché to say writers don't make good editors, but Daniel is just as brilliant a novelist as he is an editor. His genius as both is a testament to his negative capability—not bad for a straight man tackling this queer bildungsroman.

Michael Carroll, my husband, helps me in my precarious life and constant writing. He's very good at "plot-walking," which I think means divining what to write next.

My ex-student and dear friend, Cody Cortes, has been a tireless reader and encouraging long-distance companion, thanks to Skype (we live thousands of miles apart).

A NOTE ON THE AUTHOR

EDMUND WHITE is the author of many novels, including *The Humble Lover, A Boy's Own Story, The Beautiful Room Is Empty, The Farewell Symphony*, and *A Previous Life*. His nonfiction includes *City Boy, Inside a Pearl, The Unpunished Vice*, and other memoirs; *The Flâneur*, about Paris; and literary biographies and essays. He was named the 2018 winner of the PEN/Saul Bellow Award for Achievement in American Fiction and received the Medal for Distinguished Contribution to American Letters from the National Book Foundation. He lives in New York.